A NOTE FROM HANNAH

My name is Hannah, and this is the story of my life! The author, Paul Boge, has captured every inspiring and true detail of it. It certainly was not easy losing both parents and finding myself all alone with my little sister, especially because I was a girl and only a child at that. I had no hope and felt that it was the end of my life. I had no people with whom I could share my pains and thoughts, and I never dreamt I could ever achieve even one of my life goals.

Then, hope was shown to me by a man they call Daddy Mulli (Dr. Charles Mulli) and a lady called Mommy (Mrs. Esther Mulli), who are the founders of Mully Children's Family. They are my parents, whom I love so much. Since the day I arrived, Daddy and Mommy Mulli have shown me unconditional love, care, and protection in the absence of my biological parents. I know all this has been possible only through God's intervention.

At such a young age, I went through so many hardships, often feeling hopeless and with no one to take care of me, but despite all this, I never gave up. After the death of my parents left me a total orphan, I now know it was God who sent His servants Daddy and Mommy Mulli to my rescue. Daddy Mulli has been such a good father to me. He has been my mentor, and as I watched the way he responded to life's difficulties and saw where he let God bring him, it became the personal inspiration and driving force of my life.

It is my hope and prayer that as you read my story it will impact you positively and you will learn to appreciate even the little things of life and, like me, you will see that all things in life can become part of the road to shaping your future to who you want to become.

A NOTE FROM ISABELLA

Hannah's story as written in this book brings back so many fond memories. I especially thank God for my encounter with Hannah at Mully Children's Family. As friends, we lived together like sisters despite our ethnic differences. I found that our lives had so many similarities as we passed through the same kind of difficult situations as young girls and in them shared our undying love of God.

Our loving parents, Daddy and Mommy Mulli, have shown us great care and love from the very day we joined the family. They have always been on our side, especially when we needed their guidance. God has blessed them and their help to us abundantly.

Hannah's life really inspired me and showed me that if anyone trusts in God all things are possible and our past experiences do not determine our future lives.

Being brought up in MCF, I can testify that it is indeed a family where hope has been restored to the lives of the hopeless. MCF gives the best care and serves the less fortunate young people and marginalized members of our society. I am amazed how God has always provided for our family and we have never lacked anything.

I am proud to be part of the biggest family in the world.

"Hannah's story magnificently illustrates the healing power of the Mully Model that Charles and Esther Mulli have built over the last 30 years. Furthermore, Hannah's life reveals a key truth from the Gospels, that once we surrender everything and accept that God is in control—even when everything seems out of control—we can find contentment."

– Craig Steuterman
Executive Director, Mully Children's Family USA

• • •

"*Hannah's Hope* is just that. A story of hope because of God's great love for each child. A love modelled so profoundly by Mully Children's Family—Hannah's family. Having known Hannah for many years, Paul Boge brings her into the reader's home and heart to make the telling of her story so very real."

– Arvid and Ruth Loewen
Ambassadors for Mully Children's Family
and Founder of GrandpasCan

• • •

"*Hannah's Hope* is a wonderful glimpse into the life of one of the many, many destitute children that Mully Children's Family has rescued. As you read this true story you will feel that you get to know Hannah—her fears, her struggles, her hopes, and her dreams. You can picture her bunk bed, her dormitory, her classroom, her hundreds of sisters and brothers. One day you may actually get to travel to Kenya and see the love in this family, this amazing work of God. It is my privilege to have been to MCF Kenya eight times and to be on the Canadian board of Mully Children's Family. When I visit MCF Kenya and think of Charles Mulli I often think of the queen of Sheba's comments: 'It was a true report which I heard in my own land about your words and your wisdom. Nevertheless I did not believe the reports, until I came and my eyes had seen it. And behold, the half was not told me.' *Hannah's Hope* will give you a small taste of how God is at work today."

– Cathy Snowball
Board Member, Mully Children's Family Canada

• • •

"Paul Boge has a unique talent of bringing us into the world of MCF and Kenya. Paul has effectively taken one of the thousands of stories to help the world understand the personal but complex unique work of MCF, which has effectively released so much potential in so many marginalized and impoverished Kenyan children.

Having had the privilege of periodically experiencing and getting to know Hannah, Isabella, and many others of the MCF Family, through various visits in Kenya, and then reading their story, I am reminded of what kinds of miracles are happening on an ongoing basis at MCF.

Dr. Charles Mulli, Daddy for thousands, has not only created a complex system that rescues and rehabilitates but also has made the children into the largest family in the world. A family made up of many individual stories, each unique and a miracle in its own right.

This book is a must read for whoever wants to understand what impact MCF is having on individual impoverished marginalized orphaned children's lives, such as Hannah's. God's love, grace, power, and hope are made tangible through this amazing ministry.

– **Dr. David Rempel**
Professor at IUBH, Bad Reichenhall, Germany

• • •

"*Hannah's Hope* touched my heart! I have had the privilege of going to Mully Children's Family on more than one occasion and have the privilege of knowing Charles and Esther Mulli personally. But this book allowed me to see the miracle of MCF through new eyes, through a child's eyes. Paul Boge is an amazing writer and is able by his words to let you feel what Hannah felt on her journey, from the loss and privation she suffered as a small child to the elation she felt at being wanted and being welcomed into a new family, with a mom and dad who loved her.

This journey was a step-by-step process and is told in a very honest, believable way. It deals with her emotional healing and her learning to trust and share her heart again. Through watching Hannah experience life and acceptance at MCF, you experience it along with her—the love she felt from Charles and Esther, from her new sisters she shared a dorm with, from the teachers and pastors and all who served there. Behind everything at MCF, you see God's love manifested to these children, His heart reaching out to them in healing and restoration, giving them hope for the future. It's exciting to watch Hannah's personal journey with God and the way God extends His love for others through her.

Hannah's time at MCF was not without challenges, whether it was serving those in the slums of Nairobi or taking month-long exams that determined her future. You feel her fears, and they're real. You also see the steady love of Charles and Esther helping the children know that God has a purpose in all that they go through and that they are loved and valued. Hannah's story will not only inspire you but also challenge you in your own walk with God. I highly recommend it."

– **Nancy Clark**
Supporter of Mully's Children Family USA
Johns Creek, Georgia

Hannah's HOPE

A MULLY CHILDREN'S RESCUE STORY

PAUL H. BOGE

Hannah's Hope: A Mully Children's Rescue Story
Copyright ©2017 Paul H. Boge
All rights reserved
Printed in Canada
ISBN 978–1-927355–60–2 Soft Cover
ISBN 978–1-927355–61–9 E-book

Published by: Castle Quay Books
Tel: (416) 573-3249
E-mail: info@castlequaybooks.com | www.castlequaybooks.com

Edited by Marina Hofman Willard
Cover design and book interior by Burst Impressions
Printed at Essence Publishing, Belleville

Scripture quotations are taken from the NEW AMERICAN STANDARD BIBLE®, Copyright © 1960, 1962, 1963, 1968, 1971, 1972, 1973, 1975, 1977, 1995 by The Lockman Foundation. Used by permission.

Library and Archives Canada Cataloguing in Publication

Boge, Paul H., 1973-, author
    Hannah's hope : a Mully Children's rescue story / Paul Boge.

ISBN 978-1-927355-60-2 (softcover)

    1. Mulli, Hannah. 2. Orphans--Kenya--Biography. 3. Christian biography--Kenya. 4. Orphans--Care--Kenya. 5. Mully Children's Family. 6. Mulli, Charles. I. Title.

HV1346.5.B64 2017   362.73092   C2017-906007-4

CASTLE QUAY BOOKS

Mully Children's Family (MCF) is a home in Kenya founded and established by Charles and Esther Mulli in 1989 in response to the desperate needs of street children, impoverished children, and HIV/AIDS orphans. For more information, visit www.MullyChildrensFamily.org.

foreword
CHARLES MULLI

My heart is continually moved when I see how children and young mothers suffer due to a lack of nutritious food, shelter, medical care, and parental love. Their lives are characterized by insecurity, abandonment, and rejection. Orphans in particular are the most vulnerable and marginalized group in Kenya.

The plight of orphans and street children caught my attention when a group of street boys organized themselves to steal my car in Nairobi in April 1986. This incident caused me to re-evaluate how I was spending my life. Up until then I had been successful in business and thought that was how I would continue. But God used the event to work in my heart. Three years later, on November 17, 1989, God anointed me to be a father to the fatherless. Together with my wife, Esther, I began to reach out to children in Kenya and show them God's love.

Hannah's Hope is the true story of one such orphan girl, whose problem was reported to me by one of the senior officers at MCF. I organized a mission to rescue her from Kisumu near Lake Victoria, where she lived with her younger sister and her elderly, poor grandparents, who could not adequately care for their needs. Hannah and her sister were very little girls and in a state of abject poverty, and I felt it was my joy to welcome her and her sister into Mully Children's Family.

Hannah's story is like that of many other children (over 13,000) whom Esther and I have rescued and reintegrated into communities over the last 28 years. It is part of our ongoing mission to reach out to many others yet to join our "world's largest" family. This story shows the need to help the millions of others suffering around the world. I thank the Lord for Paul Boge and his passion in writing my books *Father to The Fatherless*, *Hope to the Hopeless*, and *The Biggest Family in the World* and for helping to edit *My Journey of Faith*. Paul has now written this great story of a little girl who became a daughter to Esther and me. We have seen Hannah grow through childhood to adulthood, full of determination, humility, obedience, and an ever-increasing love for God and people.

I encourage you to read this story of a girl who rose up from hopelessness to hopefulness. I trust it will encourage you to evaluate your own life as well. Without God, all things we do become nothing. Proverbs 19:17 says, "One who is gracious to a poor man lends to the LORD, and He will repay him for his good deed."

– Dr. Ev. *Charles Mutua Mulli*, PhD, HSC
Founder and CEO, Mully Children's Family

CHAPTER
one

Every person has their reason why they love the place they call home. For me, the reason I love Africa—the reason I hold the people and the land of Kenya so dear—is because everything here is exactly as it seems.

The smiles of strangers you pass on the road are genuine and deep. Villagers, as if responding to a centuries-old tradition handed down through the ages, take part in raising you as if you were their very own. The land, although at times difficult to cultivate and live off, still provides an incomparable calm with its vast expanse. Here, family is closer than the air you breathe and, of course, more important.

We have endless deserts, inspiring mountains, breathtaking valleys, and most famous of all, our captivating animals. My favourite are the giraffes—such peaceful creatures, with their long legs and necks that enable them to see life from a high and panoramic perspective that other animals do not have.

Africa is a land of unspoiled beauty. Of timeless cultures. And generations of authentic people. Nothing here pretends to be something it isn't. Africa is what it is.

And I find great comfort in things being as they appear to be.

I grew up in Umer, a small village in Nyanza Province near Lake Victoria. There's no reason for you to have heard about Umer. Few people have. It's like many other small towns all around the world, a place that holds special meaning for those of us who had the privilege of experiencing the precious moments of our early years here.

I grew up poor, but I had no reason to notice. Happy children rarely do. If someone had come up to me and told me that we were poor, I would not have understood. I suppose different people measure wealth in different ways. In my heart, we were rich because I had a mother, a father, a twin sister, and another little sister as well. I even had grandparents. And to make life more incredible than one could imagine possible, I had a place to sleep at night.

It never occurred to me I needed anything more.

Each family in the community lived in its own hut. Each parent had his or her own job. Whenever possible, we supported each other by buying from one another. Whenever we did not have enough to eat, we could ask our neighbours for help. We did the same for them whenever we were asked to share. In this way, the community looked out for each other. You had a sense of being together. You felt you belonged.

We could have had more food to eat. Nicer clothes to wear. Bigger places to live in. But it never occurred to us that we needed these things, or even that they existed.

You can't miss what you don't know.

As a young child, I loved playing hide-and-seek with my twin sister, Leah, in the cornfields. We laughed as we chased each other around the tall stalks. To us, they seemed like trees, towering high above, reaching to the skies. My mother kept a watchful eye over us while she worked as a casual labourer in the fields. She always took us with her, making a practice of living together with us in every situation. It was not until years later that I understood why keeping us close was important.

Leah and I often lay down on our backs, gazing up at the billowing clouds. The massive puffs of white filled the Kenyan sky, looking like an unending series of islands had been created from one end of the earth to the other. It caused me to wonder how out of all the wind and storms and rain, the clouds could look so perfectly organized. How order could come from something that appeared so random.

We lived in a hut made of mud walls and a mud floor. My parents and my eight–month-old sister, Zemira, slept in the only bedroom. Leah and I slept beside each other on a sheet on the floor in the living room. The thatched roof kept out the rain, mostly, and for all of this we were thankful. When heavy rains poured down, the water crept in under the walls. We laughed whenever this happened. I loved hearing the sound of her giggling as we quickly stood up and tried to lift the sheet before it got soaked. We would then pack mud against the wall to prevent the water from coming in any further. Then we would try to go back to sleep, trying hard not to laugh.

On clear nights, I looked out at the stars through the small opening between the wooden window coverings. Leah gazed out at them as well, staring in amazement at their beauty, comforted by their presence. We could often tell what was going on inside each other's minds, the way twins can when they have a special bond that enables them to know what is happening inside the other person. It was as if we could communicate without having to speak. As though we could sense each other's thoughts and feelings. It gave me comfort in having someone know me, really know me, right to the core, and love me just the way I was. I loved those evenings. The two of us looking out, enthralled by the celestial lights that seemed custom designed just for us. There was no electricity in our village. No other lights to cloud our view. So the stars filled the night in such a specific and unpredictable pattern that it seemed to me as if they were trying to tell us something—that the bright twinkling was in fact a message for us.

Those evenings seemed to last forever. And I could not imagine a better life.

• • •

One day my father had to move to Nairobi to find work as a carpenter. I felt sad to see him leave. The first night without him, we all sensed a deep emptiness. It was like we were suddenly living in a different hut and in a different village. For the first time, I discovered how much it hurt when he was gone. I felt disoriented. Unable to focus. Worried.

That evening the stars did not seem to shine as brightly. And it concerned me to think that he might not return for a long time.

There was less and less for us to eat each day, and there was not as much work to go around in our community. Without anyone explaining it to us, even at our young age we realized that my mother working in a field was not going to be enough to send us to school.

In spite of our difficulties, my mother remained happy. She had an eternal resilient smile on her face as evidence of her decision to rise above her circumstances. Her quiet lifestyle felt like an ocean of peace, making our separation from our father easier. After work, she cooked supper for the four of us. Then we played with Zemira before bed. Leah and I loved to tickle her. We laughed at every sound she made, trying our best to copy her every move. How could someone so small give us all so much joy?

Mother took her to her room for the night. Leah and I lay down on our sheet. We gazed through the partial opening through the wooden shutter and saw a clear evening. This meant a perfect view of the stars. And no rainwater coming in.

Still, if I had a choice, I would rather it poured in that evening instead of what happened.

I awoke to the sound of our baby sister, Zemira, crying. I had heard her cry before. But this time it sounded different. It was as if she knew what was going to happen.

When good things happen, time seems to stand still. But when tragedy strikes, time seems disjointed. Events flashed before my eyes like pictures taken in rapid succession. Everything that followed happened so quickly that I can't recall the order. I felt a throbbing in my throat, like an African drum pounding in my heart. Sweat formed on my forehead. Even though my head had not comprehended what was happening, in my heart I knew something had gone wrong.

The villagers, responding to the unanswered cries of my sister, came into our hut. People hurried into my mother's room, passing in front of Leah and me as if we weren't there. I stood beside Leah. Neither of us said anything. We did not have to. We both knew what we were thinking.

Even though our home in Nyanza Province was far away from the coast, it might as well have been a massive tidal wave that struck our hut that evening. It was as if the powerful, unstoppable water had crashed in through the windows and doors, smashing through our defences and sweeping us away into a disaster, and neither of us was remotely prepared to navigate our shocked souls back to freedom.

I cannot recall what happened next. The details didn't matter. Nothing else did.

My mother had passed away.

Time seemed to go slower, then stopped altogether. People cried and tried to console us. I should have been able to feel their presence, but they seemed a world away. It was as if a glass box had been built around me, separating me from everyone and everything else I knew. I felt like a distant observer of a world in which only a few short moments before I was an active participant. Now, I was on the outside looking in. Strange to be right in the middle of something and yet be so far away that I might as well have been invisible.

I felt like calling for help, but I did not know who to address or what to say. I wanted a hug, but I did not know how to ask for one. I wanted all of this to stop. To go away. To disappear. I wanted to return to what I had.

This was not right. None of it. This was the wrong dream. The wrong reality. The wrong tidal wave. I had shifted from a world of security and peace to this new place—a place I did not want to be in—one characterized by fear and uncertainty. I stood in the same hut I had always been in, and yet none of it was familiar. I looked at people I had known my whole life but could not recognize them. I heard voices I had heard since I was a child that now seemed like they belonged to strangers.

I felt like a foreigner in my homeland.

It was such a shock that everything inside me shut off. It was as if someone flicked a switch to make everything deep in my heart and mind close down, in an effort to protect me and leave intact whatever little fragment of me was still left.

Someone took the three of us in for the night. I can't remember who. I cried often. Not just with tears, but with my whole being. I saw the same in Leah. That hurt more. I did not want her to experience the same sadness going on inside of me. The two of us had shared the greatest joys. Now we were sharing the greatest sorrow. And the bond between us grew stronger in knowing we had a safe place with each other where we could share our bewilderment, confusion, and sorrow.

Father came home from Nairobi. He held us for as long as we wanted. Somehow his presence, despite the situation, brought us a sense of calm. I did not speak much. Even less than usual. He stayed with us for what I am sure was a long while, but when he said it was time for him to return to Nairobi, it felt like he had been with us only a short time. It feels that way with good parents. Especially when you are down to one.

Father got us settled in with our grandparents. They were kind and poor, like everyone else we knew. Father returned to Nairobi. He sent money back for us.

My grandparents had two huts on their property. One was similar to ours. The other hut was meant only for cooking. This is where my grandmother slept with us three children. The hut had a familiar mud floor and mud walls and a similar view outside through the wooden shutters to the evening sky. I tried to recapture what I had seen before, what I had felt before. I wanted that sense of wonder I had when I looked out at the universe and saw the twinkling in the night. But that was all strangely gone.

The stars did not look the same.

In the days and months that followed, my grandmother talked with me, with us, yet I found I was not able to respond. I wanted to speak with her. To share with her. To offload the unbearable burden that was consuming me. But part of me did not know how to do so. Inside me, a quiet child wanted to express her heart. Yet at the same time I felt such anguish, such inconsolable grief, such incomparable fear, that I was not able to reach down to draw out the bitter waters that had infected me. Everything inside my mind had become so unsettled, so unreliable, that I remained silent, fractured in my soul, shattered into pieces. Everything inside me hurt, and I longed for a place of safety. It was like being in a room full of people who are all asking you non-stop questions, and it all becomes so confusing that in the futility of trying to keep up, you just keep quiet, keep to yourself, and slowly retreat in the hopes that somehow, someway there will be someone out there who can put the world back together again for you.

CHAPTER
two

The bright sun shone in my eyes as the bus approached Nairobi. The big city. The famous capital of Kenya. Normally I would have squinted. Normally I would put my hand at my forehead to block out the rays. But this was my first time to Nairobi and I did not want to miss anything. More importantly, my sisters and I were coming to live with our father and his new wife.

And we were so curious what our new life would be like.

It had been three years since my mother's passing. Father had remarried and was now in a position to care for us. I so wanted to see him again. We all did. And our new mother, too. I felt nervous about meeting her. I wondered if she would like us. Wondered if we were going to be happy together. I wondered what it would feel like to be loved by a mother again. And to be hugged again.

Sometimes it's the smallest things in life that leave the greatest impressions.

My grandparents had done their best. Even though they had nothing, they gave everything. And while we all knew there was no future in living with them, I somehow had the feeling that their involvement in my life was not yet done.

The bus bumped as the driver tried to find a path down the pothole-filled road. Other passengers became annoyed. Me, I loved it. My sisters and I laughed each time there was a big jolt. Then it suddenly became smoother. We still felt the occasional bumps, but fewer than before. I looked out the window and saw the paved street. It was the first time I had seen something other than mud or gravel for a road.

It had been such a hot ride that when the drizzle started, the cool air that wafted through the windows was a welcomed change. We turned down another street into the city. I saw crowds of people walking, crammed together on either side of the street. I had never seen so many people in all my life.

I saw children on the street. Poor children. Dirty clothes. Alone. I found this strange. Where were their parents? And why were they dressed in such dirty clothes?

At every intersection, people ran out to the bus, offering us food. Mangos. Bananas. Passionfruit. There was a lot to eat. If you had money.

The bus reached the station. Normally, I would have been in awe at the crowds of people. Normally, I would have watched in silence, trying to absorb my new surroundings. Instead, I looked through the maze of people, searching for someone in particular. Interesting how with all the many, many people on our planet, our eyes know exactly when we see the person who ignites our heart. And for me, this was my father. I picked him out of the crowd. And in that moment, all the other people disappeared.

As our eyes connected we became full of life. We smiled. Our hearts lit up. I saw genuine, unmanufactured, joy rise within him. I felt the same in my heart. Seeing him set the world right. Gave me peace. The connection of father and daughter pulled us together where we belonged. We waved at him and hurried out of our seats and off the bus.

He hugged all three of us at the same time. I felt the reassurance that came with his arms squeezing us together. I wanted this moment to last forever. To feel the comfort that came with his love and security. The thrill of being together again made me feel like myself again. Wherever we happened to be—whether in our village, here in Nairobi, or anywhere else in the world—when we were with him, we were home.

He took us to his house—our house—and I felt the rush of nervousness and excitement that comes with experiencing something new. The house looked to be one room larger than the one in our village. I would have spent more time thinking about what that meant, but my heart and mind became consumed with wondering what I would experience inside its walls. Would she love us? Would I feel different around this mother compared with my first mother? Would I feel the same connection? Was that even possible?

Father opened the door. I walked in. I saw our new mother.

Our eyes connected. Yes? No? What did she think of us? In an instant light that had reflected off her eyes made its way into my eyes, where my mind began processing how to interpret how she felt towards me. But there are things that travel faster than light. Truth, for example. And quicker than an instant, I knew what she thought of me. And by the time my mind converted the glimmer in her eye to a feeling, my heart had already long since figured it out. I saw through the windows of her eyes into her soul.

And she was simply wonderful.

She smiled. No words were necessary. A genuine grin that made me feel warm all over. I heard the sound of her voice. It was more than just words. Words just carry meaning. But the tone of her voice revealed her compassionate, caring heart. She walked towards us. I was glad she made the effort to close the distance between us. I was too amazed—or afraid—to bridge the gap myself. She felt like the sun when it warms you up. She asked us how we were. We all said fine. She crouched down beside us so she could be level with us. That meant a lot. It's the small things that give you the biggest insight into a person. We were still children, and looking at an adult was a long way up. She reached out her arms. And then, she did it.

She hugged us.

A lot of me was worried about making the right impression. Was I the kind of child that someone other than my mother would love? Would she love me for who I was, or would I have to act a different sort of way to gain her love?

The hug she gave me told me that I did not need to worry about anything. And I admired her for loving children who were not hers by birth.

She rose to her feet and began to talk. She talked with lots of hand gestures. My sisters and I exchanged glances. We found that funny. She talked about how excited she was to see us. How much she had been looking forward to having us live with them. She talked a lot. That was fine by me. Whenever someone else was willing to do the talking, I felt at home.

I heard a noise beside me. I turned and saw a square object in the corner. It was like a picture, only the picture moved and had voices coming from it. I looked closer, wondering if perhaps there was something behind it to make it do that. I asked my father what it was. He explained it was a television. News was on.

He took us to our bedroom. All three of us would sleep in this room. I stopped in the doorway. Confused. I saw no sheet on the ground. Were the walls here so good that rain never came in? Is this why we would sleep directly on the ground? I looked around the room.

I saw beds.

Three of them.

He flicked a switch. The room suddenly became full of light. I wasn't sure which surprised me more, seeing light from electricity or seeing a bed to sleep in.

"These are for us?" I asked.

My dad crouched down beside me. He spoke into my ear. "These are for you. What do you think?"

The three of us children each put a hand on a bed, like touching them would ensure that our eyes were not imagining something too good to be real.

"I get to have my own bed?" Zemira asked.

"Yes!" my dad said.

She bent down and looked underneath her bed.

"Does anyone sleep under here?"

We all laughed. "No," my father said. "Only you on top of the bed."

My mother smiled in the doorway. I felt the thrill of being together. Like a whole new life lay before us.

• • •

That evening as we went to sleep, Father talked with us. I watched his face as he spoke. Now that all the excitement of arriving was over, I had a chance to really look at him, and he seemed tired. I wondered if he had to work longer hours to pay for all of us to be here with him. School was going to be expensive, and I wasn't sure if he had the money to pay for it.

He kissed us goodnight and tucked us in. He turned off the light. But the moon shone enough to illuminate the room. I looked over at Leah.

"We are in a bed," I said.

"And it is a good bed," Leah replied.

"Is it a long way down to the ground?" Zemira asked. Leah and I laughed.

"What is so funny?" Zemira leaned over her bed and looked down. "This is my first time in a bed, and if I roll over I might fall off." She reached down her hand and touched the ground. "This is really high off the ground."

"You will be fine," I replied. Then I stopped laughing. My sister was scared. I heard it in her voice. Saw it in her eyes. Felt it in the way her body was tensed up in the shoulders. And I, for one, should have known that when you are afraid, even the simplest things can become great obstacles.

"Zemira?" I asked. She looked at me with trusting eyes. I could tell because they were wide open. When people are suspicious or doubt you, they tend to squint just a little. But Zemira really listened. I could see right into her. I could tell she was waiting for me to give her words of hope. "Everything will be fine."

She waited. Thought. "All right," she said, lying down. "But if I fall, it will be your fault."

We giggled and eventually fell asleep.

• • •

Every Sunday, we sat together on wooden benches in a building with many other people. Usually we were near the front. A man would stand and preach to us. I am sure his words were supposed to encourage me, but they never did. I often wondered if that was his fault or mine.

People around us sang songs. I did not know the words. No one bothered to teach them to me. Still, for me, the singing could have gone on for hours. Hearing the music, even without knowing the words or being able to understand them, I felt a joy, peace, and safety that I did not experience anywhere else. In those brief moments of song, I felt put back together again. Like the fragment pieces of my heart were assembled. Something in the music provided me with the assurance that there was a place out there, somewhere, with true healing that managed to connect with me in the here and now. It provided me a glimpse into another place.

And then, just as quickly as it came, it departed as soon as the song was over, returning me to life as I had come to know it.

All of this church activity seemed important to my father. I, however, had no idea what was happening. Why were we here? Why were people dressed better today than on other days? And why were they folding their hands and bowing their heads? I wished I would have understood. Part of me thought about asking Father, but most of the time we just did what we were told to do.

One evening when my father came home from work I noticed he looked more tired. Maybe I hadn't been noticing the progression, but he suddenly seemed much more exhausted. He didn't say anything to us. Not about his energy level. But I could tell. I could tell the way he tried to smile. It wasn't as natural. He sat on his chair at the table and took the three of us in his arms.

"I love you all so much," he said, more in a whisper than in his normal tone of voice. I wasn't sure if that was because he was trying to be quiet or because he didn't have the energy to manage any more than that. "And always remember to be hard working."

The following morning we woke up to discover he had passed away.

It was the sound of our stepmother crying that woke me. People started arriving and filling our little home. I had been through this before. And it brought back memories I did not want to relive. I wanted to pretend this was not happening. That self-defence mechanism of not accepting reality is difficult to ignore. It is so much easier than facing reality.

When my mother died, I lost my bearings, my sense of direction, and the comfort of someone who loved me and who wanted my love in return. But losing both parents is indescribable. It was a complete confirmation that I was now alone. Just when I thought there might be some semblance of a normal life for us, everything was torn away. That tidal wave that crashed over us in our hut in the village when Mother passed was nothing compared to this one. This was an earthquake, a tidal wave, and a hurricane coming at us at once.

Leah, Zemira, and I stood in silence. Stunned. I felt an uneasy sense of panic rise within me. *Where will we go? Who will look after us? Will we become like those other children with the dirty clothes that we saw on the street?*

It was as if we had been torn out of the world and dropped into yet another new one where everything looked the same and yet everything felt so completely foreign. It didn't feel like we were in the right place. It was as if something had taken hold of me and gripped me with such grief, such fear, such sadness that I was powerless against it.

In losing Mother, I had the relief of knowing that Father was going to come and that he would make it all all right.

And he had. For a while.

But who exactly was going to make it right now?

No one had to tell me my situation now. No one had to explain it to me or to my sisters. I knew it all too well.

I was an orphan.

If I was quiet after Mother passed away, I was completely silent now. I was unable to speak to our neighbours when they took us in that evening. I wanted to say something to our stepmother, who simply cried uncontrollably, yet I was not able to say any words of encouragement to her. I wondered why she was crying so much. It looked like more than grief. The intensity of her crying made me wonder if she felt in some way responsible for his illness.

I didn't take notice of our neighbour's house. Normally I would have studied the home and observed everything that made it unique. I suppose I didn't care, because I knew we would be leaving and going back to our impoverished life with my grandparents.

I thought about my father that entire day and night and for many weeks and months ahead. How exactly can you go from seeing a person the night before to the person being completely gone the next day? How does that happen? Why is that when they are gone they still feel like they are very much alive and that at any moment they are going to come through the door and give you a hug?

Not only had I lost two people that I knew, but I lost two people who knew me. And it was in the not-being-known that I felt my greatest loss. I found it ironic to be on a continent with so many people and yet feel so completely and thoroughly alone.

I sat there that night with my two siblings. The three of us, alone in our new bedroom. It felt so strange. None of us had any idea what to do.

In the days and weeks and months that followed we were shuffled about, cared for by many. Yet it was from here to there to there to here, and in the end I did not know where here or there was anymore.

Nobody ever warned me that grief is the same as fear. I was scared, but I did not know why or what I was scared of. There is something about losing everything that makes you feel you are living alone in the dark. Even the bright African sun did nothing to lift the eternal fog of our hearts and minds. I felt I had returned to the dream I experienced after my mother's passing. I was looking at life in slow motion. I could see people but not relate to them. Hear them, but not interact.

Grief does strange things to people. Especially to us as children.

We travelled back to our village for the funeral. I stood at the gravesite of my father. I was later told there were many people at the burial site. But at the time, all I could see was the end of my parents. All I heard was the unbearable sound of deafening silence.

And all I felt was the stinging realization that all of this was real.

Afterwards came the debate over who would get to look after us. As awkward as it is to have your fate discussed after a funeral, it was comforting to know how much we were wanted. In the end our grandparents won out over our stepmother. I loved them all very much, and if there would have been a way to have us all together I suppose that would have been best. Our stepmother gave us farewell hugs. I missed her immediately. I admired how she loved us.

We settled back in with our grandmother. Strange how at such a young age I had already gotten used to being moved around so much. It was life, and when you are young you don't know what to compare it to, so you just presume it is normal.

It did not take long for Leah and me to wonder—*worry* would be more accurate—about our future. Our grandparents had no money, and without money we weren't going to school. And without school we would not get a decent job, and without a decent job we would be forced to do whatever manual labour we could find.

Not long after our return, Grandmother informed us we would be going to school. Leah and I were ecstatic. Then surprised.

How would our grandmother afford to send us?

As I went to sleep, on the mud floor, on the sheet, I wondered about studying, wondered where it would all lead, wondered what the end result of all my studying would be. Would I be able to go to university one day? And if so, what kind of career or job would I like to have? What would I like to do? What would I like to become? I let my mind wonder and paid no attention to the normal restrictions of life. I didn't care if I could afford it. I didn't care if it seemed impossible. I wanted to escape to a place where I could just dream. Just imagine. Just step into the clouds and believe that whatever was on my heart could become reality.

And for the first time, I realized what my heart's desire was.

CHAPTER
three

It should not have been possible.

Many people had tried and failed. Yet my grandmother convinced the teacher to let us attend school without any money. In Kenya, all children are required to pay for school. On top of that, we have to pay for uniforms. We could not even feed ourselves, yet we were expected to climb out of poverty by obtaining an education we could not afford.

I was down to one meal a day. We all were. The word *meal* itself is a relative term. What is a meal exactly? Is it when you eat until you are full? Or could it also refer to the small portions of rice my grandmother sacrificed everything for? When we first came back to our grandparents I often wondered what it would be like to eat three times a day again like we did with our father. But the longer I stayed here, the more I found myself being grateful for the one meal we could have together. Even if it was so little. I had to learn to shift my expectations of life. No doubt I wanted three meals a day. I needed three meals a day. But life is what life is, and I found it was better to try to focus on what I did have than to focus on what was missing.

The hunger pangs left me debilitated. It was as if someone had sucked the energy from my veins. My stomach felt different pains at different times of the day. The hungrier I got, the worse I felt. I often wondered what I would do if Grandmother would not be able to provide. I could not come up with any solutions.

I often felt tired, weak. I would lie down on the mud floor in the afternoon, thinking how much I would love to play with the other children. But playing takes energy. And even at a young age I had to learn how to ration what little strength I had.

Leah found it even more difficult. I sensed something different in her. She walked slower than I did. We encouraged each other to lie down and would look into each other's eyes, hoping to rest. Sleep is a great way to pass the time. Or to avoid it altogether.

We had no money. No chickens. No goods with which to barter. The sum total of everything we had was nothing. And yet Grandmother took us to the schoolyard. To the teacher. To hope for a miracle.

"God will provide," she told me.

I wondered about that. Exactly how would the same God who allowed my parents to die provide for me to go to school? Grandmother had faithfully knelt down, even at her old age—I will never forget that picture of humility—and prayed to God for help.

The school here in the village looked different than schools we saw in Nairobi. City schools were made of bricks. Here, the walls were made of mud. The wooden desks looked older. The classrooms were small and cramped. None of this mattered to me, though. I would have gone to school in the open pouring rain if it meant I could have a chance at a better life.

In Nairobi, we sometimes managed to stay in school until the end of the first month. But when the teachers discovered we could not pay the fees, they would get rid of us. I wondered how long it would take them to figure that out here.

Grandmother walked ahead of us to the playground. She approached a teacher and began to speak with her. I was thankful she did not take us with her. This way, when the teacher found out we could not pay, it would be a simple shake of her head instead of escorting us out in full view of all the others.

I watched the children play hide-and-seek and especially football (what people in other parts of the world refer to as soccer). I wondered what it would feel like to run with all the others, to be with such a large group of children. I wondered what it would feel like to fit in.

Grandmother returned. I looked in her eyes for any hint of direction as to what would happen next.

"You can go to school," she said in way that seemed she had known all along this would happen.

I stood still, as if I were a tree, unable to believe what I had just heard. It felt unique to experience shock over good news. Amazing news, actually.

Or was it?

Would this last? Did Grandmother pay her money? Would the money run out? I did not see any money change hands. I was sure of it. I swallowed. My stomach growled. I ignored the pain. I am not sure what surprised me more, that I was actually going to school or that my grandmother had been expecting this all along.

"Thank you," I said. Leah and I hugged her.

"All right. All right," she said. "Get going. She is waiting for you. And study hard."

Leah and I stepped onto the school ground. It felt different, like we were trying to decide if we belonged or were only visitors.

The teacher called all the children into the classroom. We hurried to catch up. As we approached I saw the expression on the teacher's face. Her smile, her eyes, her whole being—every part of her exuded such joy. In just that short instant, she put me at ease. Some people have that gift. She motioned with her hands for us to go inside.

Leah and I stopped at the doorway. I felt the gazes of the other children as we entered. I wondered what they were thinking. They all seemed so smart, so put together. Like they had been doing this for years.

I wished someone would say something. Their silence made my awkwardness ten times worse. We were only the centre of attention for a few seconds, but to me it felt like hours. I glanced up. I saw openings near the ceiling that let the warm air escape to keep the classroom cool. Part of me wished I could be as invisible as that air.

Two students sat at each desk. There were no empty desks, not entirely, so the teacher directed Leah and me to sit at different desks next to other students. It was an adjustment. I had assumed that my twin and I would sit together. It felt strange to be apart from her.

It was not until we walked on the concrete surface to our desks that it occurred to me why some of the children stared. It was not that we were new. Not because we were twins. (Most thought we were sisters a year apart, until we told them otherwise.) They stared at us because they felt sorry for us. We reminded them of where they once were. They stared because we did not have shoes.

Being without shoes at our huts did not bother us. No one else had shoes. Not the kids, anyway. It never occurred us that something might be wrong with going barefoot to school. We wanted shoes. Every child does. You could offer a poor African child any gift they want, suggesting a giraffe, an elephant, a zebra, the moon. Anything. Yet the answer would always come back the same—a pair of shoes.

I sat down at my desk, and Leah sat at hers. We glanced at each other for reassurance, the way sisters do when their bond connects them even if they are separated by distance. The teacher wrote on the chalkboard. Everyone focused their attention on what she taught. And Leah and I blended in, just like the way I wanted us to.

It was both fun and challenging to be in the classroom. I felt excited to learn. But I found it hard. Very, very hard. Many things I did not understand. When the morning finished, the teacher encouraged me, telling me I would get used to it, even if at first I felt in over my head. As I walked out, I knew something about being here resonated with me. I felt hope in learning, in pursuing an education, in believing my future could be different than my past.

At lunchtime we stepped outside into the bright sunshine. I blinked as my eyes adjusted. Some of the children ran to play football. I admired them running in the heat like that. Others sat under the shade of trees and played games while eating lunch.

Leah and I stood listening to our stomachs growl. I turned to the girl who sat next to me in school. She was kind. She was smart. She was short.

She had food.

She sat cross-legged on the ground, eating ugali, and she had lots of it. Ugali is white crushed corn. It is a famous Kenyan food. Everyone eats it.

I was too shy at first to ask her to share. I felt bad for hoping for some of her lunch when in fact it might well have been the only meal she would have that day. Or even the next.

I think she sensed I was going to ask her for something to eat. She turned to me.

"Could I have some of your lunch?" I asked, hoping she had the courage to turn me down if she did not have enough.

It felt like an eternity to hear her answer. I felt so vulnerable. Part of me felt it would be easier to go without food. But better to be humble and fed than proud and hungry.

She did not answer. Not with words. She smiled and handed us her ugali. I thanked her as I broke off a piece. I chewed the soft maize. I swallowed. I felt the calm that came with knowing my stomach was looked after. She invited us to join her. We did. We talked, laughed, and did the things children do when they don't have to worry about their basic needs.

And it made me realize how powerful it is to simply reach out to someone and love them.

We ran home barefoot that afternoon, the skin on the bottom of our feet having long since become tough from grinding against the roads and hard surfaces. Now that we were with family, it felt natural to be without shoes.

"How was school?" Grandmother asked as we entered the door. I smelled a fire cooking. Two meals in one day.

Two.

"It was good," I said.

"When do I get to go?" Zemira asked.

I bent down and gave her a tight squeeze. "You get to go to school when you are big," I said.

She opened her mouth wide in shock. Then she said, "I am already big!"

"You are?"

"Yes, I am."

"But are you really big?"

"Yes."

"Too big for a hug?"

I tickled her. She wiggled in that way children do when they both love to be tickled yet at the same time try to get away.

"Let's go play," she said.

"In a minute," Grandmother said. "Leah and Hannah, tell me more about school."

Leah talked about the classes, about the students, about eating maize. She shared with her all the excitement of our first day.

Grandmother glanced at me. "Hannah?"

"It was good," I said, smiling with my mouth but not with my eyes. Anyone can smile with their mouth. But only a joyful heart can smile through a person's eyes. And she saw this.

"It was good?"

She tilted her head to let me know she could tell something was not right. She was too perceptive to let words get in the way of meaning. So she asked me more questions. I gave more answers. And with each reply I felt myself opening up to her. Part of me tried to forget what was bothering me. But Grandmother, in her calm way, kept talking with me. She understood me better than I understood myself.

"You can tell me," she said. Leah and Zemira hurried outside. It was fun to see them play. Grandmother and I sat down outside our door on old wooden chairs. I felt the comfort people feel when you know the other person is patiently waiting for you to speak, giving you time to collect your thoughts. I looked out at Zemira and Leah. Then I turned to Grandmother. I had a hard time meeting her glance so I looked down at the ground at my bare feet.

"I feel bad," I said. And the moment I said that, I felt bad for feeling bad.

"It is all right."

"It is not all right. I ..."

"Why do you feel bad, Hannah?"

I exhaled. "I feel bad because I don't have what the other children have." I then felt even worse, because Grandmother had just helped us get into school, and now here I was complaining.

She did not reply. Not right away. She nodded in a way that conveyed she understood. Her presence alone gave me the freedom to share.

"The other children have shoes, and we do not. And ..." I wanted to continue. But it was as if there was a competing side to me that wanted to close up, to shut down and not let anyone in. "And when I see the other children, it ..."

Don't say it. Don't trust anyone with your feelings. They are for you and you alone.

But I want to share. I need to share. Who else can I turn to? Who else can I talk to?

You don't need to share. You are strong. You are capable. You do not need this.

But I feel all confused in my mind.

Do you see what your grandmother did? She gave you schooling. And now look at you.

"Yes?" Grandmother asked in a way to encourage me to continue.

Everything swirled around inside my mind.

Just keep everything to yourself. No one will understand if you try to explain.

I fought the negative voice in my head and shared my feelings. "When I see other children who are succeeding or who have shoes or who have food, I feel like I am not as good. That I have failed … That I don't belong."

I felt that comfort that came with speaking openly with her. Sometimes when you share your heart, you don't need advice. You just need to feel you have been heard. This is how I felt with her.

"Be encouraged," she said. "Even if others have more, don't give up. Don't ask 'why do I not have that?' Just thank God for everything He has given to us. He has a blessing for us. God has a purpose for everything, and one day He will really provide everything."

I felt my heart change. Her words made sense. And from that moment, whenever we saw children with shoes and we still had to go around barefoot, we did not feel bad.

Not at all.

• • •

On Saturdays, Grandfather woke us up early in the morning to help on the farm, *shamba* in our language, Swahili. He worked hard and believed that teaching us to work would help us throughout our lives. We used a wooden tool with a small metal piece at the end called a *jembe* to till the ground by hand. If I thought time could stand still when students stared at me, it certainly stood still when we worked under the hot African sun.

In the evenings, Grandfather loved to tell us jokes. He told the best stories. We sat together in our tiny hut, laughing and laughing. Even though we lacked food, we carried on with life. None of us felt bad about not having much. We had each other. What else did we need? I do not recall even one time when any of us were angry.

Grandfather would also turn on the radio. We sang together. He clapped for me, telling me I was a great singer. In our little hut, I developed a love for music, under my grandparents' watchful encouragement.

Those evening are great memories. I loved those times when my grandparents, my two sisters, and I spent time together. We had nothing, and yet we had everything. There was something so pure about not needing more things to be really content and happy. Had I known it then, I probably would have cherished them even more.

Perhaps it would have helped me more for what lay ahead.

CHAPTER
four

Having a twin is like having a second version of yourself. Leah and I often found ourselves thinking the same thoughts at the same time. So many times we shared emotions, thoughts, and reactions. When I was happy, she was happy. When I was sick, she was sick. We were the same in so many ways.

As similar as we were, I was able to attend school more often than she was. We ate the same amount of food, slept the same amount of time, and did the same activities. But Leah became more and more tired. She would stay home while I went to school.

I felt a sharp pain in my stomach as I walked to school one day. What used to be a short walk now felt like a long journey. The hot sun beat down on me as I lifted each foot. Each step felt like incredible effort, like the way an exhausted runner might feel nearing the end of a marathon if she hasn't had enough water or training.

I reached the schoolyard. It should have been a time for playing games. Instead, I felt like collapsing. I wanted to reach the classroom, but not finding the energy I simply sat down, waited for the announcement that class would start, and watched the other children.

I often enjoyed observing people. But in recent times I found myself becoming preoccupied with thinking about other people's lives and, increasingly, my own life. What was once a positive reflection on life now became dominated by an ongoing fight to remain hopeful. Things that did not used to bother me now consumed my thoughts. I had no defence against the onslaught of negative thinking. It was as if a voice inside my head suddenly had free range to attack me, and I was sapped of any energy to fight against it.

These children have food to eat. You don't. You don't even have parents. They do.

And try as I might, I just could not find it within me to be rid of this voice.

Your grandparents are poor. You will end up just like them. Your life will be poverty and hunger. You don't even have the illusion of a brighter future because even the most optimistic person on earth would see that you are a starving orphan.

It all seemed so logical. So factual. Who was I kidding? Who were any of us kidding? No food. No parents. No money. No future.

Of the many difficulties in African life, giving in to the realization that life cannot improve is among the hardest.

I made it to class. I was last. The others had run in ahead of me. I sat down at my desk. The teacher told us to open our books. The others flipped the pages and got to the right place, but it seemed like my mind was in a deep fog, like I knew what to do but lacked the power to do it. I looked at my hand and thought, *Okay, pick up the book and get on with it.* But it took all my effort to move my hand to the cover and flip the pages. As the teacher spoke I fought to concentrate on her. I found my mind drifting, like a leaf on the river that goes wherever the rushing water takes it.

Will there be enough food at lunch? Will there be any food? Can we grow more crops? Can I find food in the—

"Hannah, what do you think?" the teacher asked.

I had no idea. She had taken me in because I was poor, and the least I could do was concentrate. And I was. As best as I knew how.

"I ..." I said as my eyes tried to focus on her. I raised my eyebrows to get the teacher to become one image instead of the three I was seeing. "I am not sure." It was a safe response. Hard to give the right reply when all you feel like doing is falling into a deep sleep.

I went home for lunch. On the way, I wondered what the point of that was. Would I get enough food to even warrant the trip there and back to school? Wasn't I better off just staying at school, resting, and then coming home and having what little I would have had at lunch for supper instead?

I managed to make it home that day.

Unfortunately.

Leah had stayed back from school. That was nothing new. What was new was the crowd of people around our hut. We didn't have crowds of people around our hut. Not at normal times.

I came closer and heard people crying. I began to cry. I knew what had happened. I did not need to be told. Twins always know. Somehow we just do.

I felt so empty all of a sudden. Like I was there but at the same time in a completely different world. People moved about me as if in slow motion. For a moment, I felt like backing up and walking off the property as if doing so could undo what had happened. I wished that maybe I could avoid all of this and pick a different path to follow, one where my twin and I could walk through life together.

But the realization of her passing began to work its way through my dark skin and into my heart. I felt a sting of tears begin to well up around my eyes, which then streamed down my face. This was not how life was supposed to work. It just wasn't.

My grandmother saw me, ran to me, and hugged me. My grandfather came out and wrapped me in his arms as well. I tried to look past them for my younger sister, Zemira. And when I saw her sitting outside I felt the strangest sense of wanting to grab on to her. She saw me through the haze of people, and in that moment before she got up and came over to me our eyes connected in a way that we had not experienced before.

How strange that we were once seven, and now we were down to four.

• • •

That night, I lay down on the ground next to my only remaining sister. We looked into each other's brown eyes. There was a knowing with her as well. Not the same as I had with Leah, of course, but we understood each other. It was deep, yet different. She fell asleep first. I was glad for that. It is better when the younger ones fall asleep first. Somehow, young children believe that the other person will remain up the whole night, keeping a watchful eye over them.

Heaven knew we needed someone looking out for us.

I remained quiet that evening, and many evenings thereafter. I would stare up at the blank ceiling or out at the stars. Every day I felt like I was carrying heavy pails of water on my shoulders. The world around me felt like it was spinning so fast, and I was no longer able to keep up. I understood nothing of what was happening in my life.

• • •

The students at school would not mention Leah's name. Not to me. There was a strange silence that seemed to envelop me. They thought that if they talked to me about my sister's passing, something bad would happen to me as well. As if the malnutrition that had taken her life could somehow be transferred into my body just by the mention of her name. Walking in that odd quiet among the students made me feel as though I was not really there, like I was invisible and unable to interact with people who were close enough to touch.

I sat at my desk and tried to focus on the chalkboard. Out of the corner of my eye I saw the empty spot where Leah had sat. I tried to listen to the teacher. I don't know how much sank in. Probably not much; grief and hunger make it difficult to concentrate.

When class ended, I felt my pulse quicken. Children stood and hurried for the door. But a sudden panic gripped me. I felt like crawling under the desk and staying there.

Come on. You have to stand up. You can do it. Just go to the door.

I cannot.

But you can. It's all right.

I am just going to wait here.

For how long? School is over. Come, you need to go.

I … I don't know what to do. I just want to sit here.

The teacher said something to me. I didn't hear the words, but the tone was kind. I slid one of my bare feet into the aisle and managed to stand. I walked to the door, and despite the bright, sunny day, I had the feeling it would be safer to stay inside. Even though there was no evidence for it, there seemed to be a large storm brewing for no one else but me, and I should remain at my desk, just to be sure.

I forced myself to step outside. The children played football and jump rope. Some looked like they were laughing and singing, but I could not hear their voices. It was as if the sound of life had been turned off.

I did not want to walk home. Not alone. It was a long way back. Wasn't it? How far was it exactly between school and home? It seemed a lifetime ago when I could walk there and back without a thought about the distance. Now it consumed me.

I managed to make it to our hut and sat down on a small stool. There was homework to do. There were chores. There were games to be played.

Yet I sat there and sat there, thinking to myself that the only safe thing in the world was for me to stay right there.

Grandmother sat down next to me. She put her arm around me and did not say anything for a while. She did not need to. Some people understand with words. Others just by being there. I felt relieved she was at my side, even though I was not sure how to communicate my gratitude to her. It seemed to me our hut was all that was left of my world. I did not want to go outside again. Not ever. I simply wanted to stay there. The world outside my front door that I once knew and loved had become a distant planet I would never again be able to reach.

She gently rocked me side to side. It was so gradual, so still, that if you were looking from a distance you would not be able to tell that we were moving.

"God loves you," she said.

I had heard this before many times during our visits to church each Sunday. Hearing about God's love is one thing when life is going well, but it seemed to mean something different when things had fallen apart. It was as if someone were trying to build a connection inside me between a loving God and a life of difficulty.

"He has a good plan for your life," she continued. In my heart, I sensed that what she was saying was right. But any kind of life other than this just felt so impossible in my mind that I wondered how any of what she was saying could come to pass.

"It is not easy to understand when people die. Yet God has made it possible for you to live." She stopped and waited for me to look up. "You can trust God, Hannah. Even in this."

Was that really possible? Was the God I heard about in church a real God I could trust despite so many difficulties in my life? And if I were to trust Him, what was I trusting Him for? Was I waiting on Him for a life of only good things and comfort? Or was there something more … something deeper?

"I want to encourage you to let your worries go. To give it all to Him. To leave it all in His hands."

There was not much I could leave in God's hands. I had nothing to give. Not any good things anyways. My life was all that I had. And it surprised me to know He wanted it.

"I love you," she said. "And you should not feel alone."

She stayed beside me until she sensed it was okay to go. I am not sure how she knew that exactly. But when she stood to go, the timing felt right. She walked out the door. I admired that—her ability to stand up and turn the door handle and to go out into the world.

I reflected on her words—what she said about God and His love for me. I thought about putting my trust in God. I thought about how I did not have many other options. I did not have the strength to do anything on my own. I had no idea how life was supposed to go on.

I was at the end.

In our little hut, on our little property, I folded my small hands. I did not have the energy to ask God for anything. I was not entirely sure that I should. So, I prayed the best I could from my confused heart and worried mind. "Let Your will be done, God," I said. "Anything that happens, I just let You take control."

The room felt different in that moment. Fuller. Like there were suddenly many people inside that empty place. I was done with wishing my life could be different. I was powerless to change anything, and yet somehow it seemed like a faint glimmer of hope had returned, like the small sliver of light that had managed to make its way through the crack at the bottom of the door had now filled the room with light.

I stood up. I walked to the door. I reached out my hand. I touched the handle. I took in a breath. I opened the door. A gust of wind blew past me. I felt the sunshine on my face.

And heard my sister Zemira calling out for me to join her in a game of skipping.

CHAPTER
five

I had a hard time deciding.

I wondered if I should gather the courage to commit to a dream that had been growing in my heart. Or should I just dismiss it as the fanciful wishes of a girl in a desperate situation? Dreams are fine. But dreams can be dangerous if we are not sure where they have come from. They can become idols that are not possible to reach, and we can trick ourselves into thinking we are designed for something that we were never meant to achieve. Yet in my heart, right at my very core, I sensed a deep conviction.

I had seen so much suffering. The passing of my parents and my twin sister caused me so much grief, so much worry, that the very thought of talking about it, or even needing to, had completely escaped me.

I could not get my parents back. I could not get my twin sister back. That much I knew. And I had grown wise enough to resist the temptation of wishing for a different past. Still, if I was not to be spared the pain of losing so much, then perhaps I could be used to help spare someone else from losing so much. What could I do to intervene in the life of someone else to spare him or her the grief I had to endure?

Life could have been so different if my parents and sister had lived, like the way a football game changes in a close match when the ball strikes the post and goes in instead of bouncing back. And if I was honest, I knew that medical intervention could have saved them. My sister and parents would have still been there had there been medical help and healthy food.

I stood outside our hut looking out at the distant horizon, at that place far away where the land meets the sky. Thinking. Praying. Wondering.

Forget it! This is impossible!

But it is on my heart.

So what? Look at your schooling.

I can accomplish it.

You will never make it.

Yes, I will. I refuse to believe that it cannot be done.

You will eventually give up.

No. I will not. I will not dishonour them. I have the faith to believe the impossible.

And how will this happen exactly? … You see. You don't know.

I don't have to know. I have faith.

I did not want to see past my own hurts. I did not want to pretend they did not exist. I wanted to use them. I wanted to use the experiences I had to pass through for the benefit of others. I could not undo what had been done. I could not help my own past. Neither could I help the pasts of others. But what about the future?

What if I could be used to help others like me? What if I could help prevent their pain? What if there was a way that I could be used to intervene in people's lives, children's lives, to prevent them from having to go through what I went through? What would they need? How could I serve them?

And it was at that moment that I decided I wanted to become a doctor.

Part of me wanted to believe against all odds that this dream would become reality. That I could become a doctor. That I could break free from the shackles of poverty to do for others what was not done for me.

But the other part of me was afraid to believe. Afraid that a poor girl without parents or money would not have any chance to go to school. I was afraid of the hard work involved and that I would only prove to myself I was a failure. If I chased this dream and it did not work, I would never again have the luxury of escaping my life through the belief that dreams could come true.

These two voices collided inside my head.

I can do it. I can become a doctor. I can learn skills to heal the sick.

Impossible. You? A doctor? Why don't you pretend to become a princess or a billionaire or an astronaut while you are at it?

It can happen.

Sure, it can happen. And maybe the world will stop spinning. Maybe the sun will turn blue. Maybe all the animals in Africa will grow wings and start to fly. Get this clear in your mind: giraffes will fly before you become a doctor. And elephants, too.

It is in my heart. And I have a passion for helping others. For seeing them become better.

That is admirable. Really it is. Everyone should want that. But not everyone can do something about it. You are one of them. Rich children do good things like that. Poor children do not.

That is not true.

But it is. You have no money. No money means no school. No school means no university. No university means not becoming a doctor. This is not about being cruel. It is only about being realistic. And your dream is not realistic.

But it is. I know that it is. Somehow there will be a way. And I will be used to help others. I don't care about money.

The school sure will.

I don't care about the odds.

A thousand rich children in Kenya are all ahead of you.

And I don't care about dreams being achievable or not. What is in my heart will be real. And I pray to God that He will make it so.

It felt strange. Awkward, really. To suddenly have a vision. A goal. A dream. It was like wearing someone else's shoes. It felt too big, and yet it felt part of me.

That evening I lay down on my sheet on the floor. I listened to the sounds of Africa at night. I heard the crickets chirping. They sounded like a symphony of a large number of musicians providing a loud sound that seemed to alternate between one side of our hut to the other. I heard the occasional grebe bird calling out, like it was looking for a friend. I smiled when I heard an owl hooting. They lived the opposite time compared to us. I could not imagine sleeping during the day and being awake all night. Their sounds comforted me, as if they were echoing the desires of my heart. Normally I would have been able to fall asleep listening to them, but that evening I found it difficult. I lay on my side with my head resting on a small pillow. How was I going to get enough money to get through school and university? Grandmother was able to convince the teacher to let me in for free, but how long would that last? For my entire schooling? What happens when a young girl in Kenya has a big dream and no means to reach it?

I felt the gentle calm that comes with beginning to drift off to sleep. It was as if someone were there beside me, laying their hand on my forehead.

I heard a knock at the door.

I recognized it.

Grandmother went to answer. But even before she reached the door, I knew who would be standing there. The knock was so quiet and playful. It could only be one person.

Grandmother opened it. There stood a medium-sized man with a kind, gentle demeanour. He laughed and raised his eyebrows. It was as if he brought a gust of wind with him wherever he went that created joy. I felt good when I saw him. I always did.

"Uncle Raza," I said as I stood.

"Hello, hello, hello. How are you?" He hugged me, then reached out to hug Zemira, who ran up to him. "I would like to know, how is it that you two girls keep getting bigger and bigger each time I see you? I thought we had talked about you staying exactly the same height from here on in? Why are you getting so tall?"

"That's because we're growing!" Zemira said.

"Growing? How high will you grow? Even taller than me?"

Zemira smiled and nodded her head.

"Really?" he continued. "Well then, I will be the one to look up to you!"

We all laughed. He reached down to tickle us. We giggled as we squirmed in his arms. Grandmother invited him in. He sat down on the end of the couch, Zemira and I beside him. Grandmother offered him chai tea to drink, which he politely declined. He must have been thirsty.

Even though it was evening, it was still hot, and with the long walk there he must have needed something to quench his thirst, but he would not take from us. Not anything. He was not one who took things.

"I would like to share some news with you," he said as he looked at Zemira and me.

Did he find a new job? Did he have a new place for us to live?

"I have been thinking a lot about you two and what kind of a future you will have. You are in school, but I wonder for how long."

I wondered the same thing.

"Your wonderful sister Leah and your parents are no longer with us. And you have many basic needs. Food, clothing, shelter, education. Grandmother is doing the very best she can." He looked up at her in a way that conveyed that he admired and respected her self-sacrifice for us. "But it is quite a large burden. And you both have so much potential."

I became curious about where all of this was leading. His honesty made it easy to see the excitement he had in sharing what was on his heart. And I wondered what it was.

"There will be many challenges. And without parents, it will be difficult for you two girls to advance much further. It is not much of a life, but …"

I held my breath. The hut became quiet. If the birds were still making noises outside, I no longer heard them.

"But things can be different," he said.

I waited in silence. I suddenly believed that he held a key to unlock the door to a brand-new future. But how? What was so urgent that he had to come this late in the evening? What was so important that it could not wait until morning? I wondered what he was going to bring us. And while it may have only taken a moment for him to continue, for two young girls hanging on his every word it felt like a long time.

I watched his excited eyes. I felt hope rising with each second inside the hut. It was like a balloon that gets bigger and bigger and you wonder when it is going to explode. I waited for him to deliver the news.

And then it came.

"I was wondering," he said. "Have any of you ever heard of Mully Children's Family?"

CHAPTER
six

There is power in words. Not simply in what is said, but in the assurance behind certain phrases spoken at certain times by certain people that can provide great encouragement. Especially to people in need. Especially to me.

A word spoken at the right time changes everything.

I had never heard of Mully Children's Family. Yet the simple sound of those three words somehow—somehow—convinced me right to my core that this was a place of hope. How could that be? How was it possible to know in my spirit that this was a good place even though I had never been there? It was just a name. Wasn't it? Or maybe my inner being was so grasping for any semblance of positive news that no matter what my uncle would have said I would have automatically assumed it was good.

No, it was more than desperate hope. After hearing those words part of me came alive. It was as if I had always been longing to hear them—like this was an appointment that had been set years ago. This was not something that only affected my mind and heart. Those three words spoke right to my spirit. And I knew in the deepest place where any person knows things to be true that this was a place for me.

Mully Children's Family.

"I have not heard of it," I said. That was true. But if that were so, why did I have such an unmistakable connection with a place I had never heard of?

"Let me tell you," he said, hardly able to contain himself. "I work at Mully Children's Family. It is a home with hundreds of children. And it is run by a man named Charles Mulli."

I felt a rush of peace come over me. For the first time in a long while I felt I could breathe again. Like something had released its tight grip on me. I felt I was living a dream from the night before. Who was Charles Mulli? I had no idea. Absolutely none. Still, I felt I had known him my entire life.

"There are amazing people in this world. But no matter where you go—whether you go high up in the mountains or get on a plane or a boat and go all around this world, I tell you—and now you really have to listen to me—you will not find such a man as this. Charles Mulli—he is a fascinating man. You can even walk to every city and country and continent in this whole earth and you will not meet a man like him."

As I listened to our uncle in our humble home, I knew I was hearing words I would never forget. I knew I would look back years in the future and always remember where I was and what I was doing when I first heard the name Charles Mulli.

I think many people would tell you the same thing.

"When he was just six years old, his family abandoned him," Uncle continued. "Left him all alone. Can you imagine? He wakes up one morning and they are all gone. He has nothing. He has to go from hut to hut with his hands outstretched, begging for food."

I could relate to asking for food. That feeling of a knot in your stomach, tired eyes, difficulty concentrating, and having to find it within you to hold out your hands for something to eat. Knowing that this man Mulli also had to beg gave me immediate comfort. I felt he could understand what I went through.

"He was not able to attend school, because he lacked the required fees. That left him with no education, no money, and no family. All he could do was dig holes for a little bit of money to help him survive. Everything looked completely hopeless."

My sister Zemira leaned in to me. I instinctively put my arm around her.

"But one day, when he was a teenager, a friend invited him to a church gathering. He heard about God, and he received real hope. When he was older, God gave him an idea to start a business driving a taxi. That business grew bigger and bigger. He branched out into other businesses. Oil and gas. Property management. Insurance. He got married, had a family, and became so rich, right here in Kenya, that he could buy anything that he wanted."

I tried to imagine that. What would it be like to be able to buy anything you wanted? What did *anything* look like? For me, my imagination took me as far as a pair of shoes, enough food for two days—maybe even a week—and a bed to sleep in. I could not ask for or even imagine more than this. And yet this man Charles Mulli had far exceeded what I could not even dream of.

The passion in my uncle's voice told me he was speaking about a man who had affected his life far beyond anyone else on this earth. Even if I had suddenly become deaf, I would still have been assured of what he was telling us. He motioned with his hands and his arms with such fervour. His eyes shone bright with hope. Joy comes with sharing good news. But this was a joy I had not seen before. He conveyed a larger reality, a truth, something so deep that it would make all other pursuits plain by comparison.

"And even with all of his money, he felt convicted in his heart about the many children here in Kenya who have no parents. Children who walk the streets. Who have no place to call home."

My uncle described a man who once had to beg and who now loved children like me who had no parents. At first, this amazed me. But the more I thought about it, the more it concerned me. I had nothing to offer him. No money. No goats. No sheep. What did all the other children have that I did not have? What did it take for them to be rescued? What did he require of those children to come to his home?

This all suddenly became impossible and pointless. We could not afford school. Certainly we would not be able to afford living in this man's home.

"He struggled with what he should do. He thought 'Do I stay in business, or do I help all these children?' He felt a deep love for children who had no food, who had no family—children who had been just like he had been. But how would he help them? And then one day everything changed for him and hundreds of others."

Hundreds? Is that what he said? How exactly was a rich man going to help hundreds of people? Would he buy them food? Would he help them to go to school? How can one man do such a thing?

"One day Charles Mulli came out of a business meeting and discovered his car had been stolen by street children. That got his mind thinking about the street children problem. And after much praying he wanted to do something to help. But what? What should he do?"

That was easy. A rich man should give some of his money to help those children. Give them food. Maybe a place to stay. It seemed so obvious to me.

But wouldn't his money eventually run out? What rich person would do that? Wasn't the point of becoming rich to also stay rich?

"He left his office one day feeling very sick. And on his way home he became disoriented. Confused. He pulled over on the side of the road and discovered he had been driving in the wrong direction. Can you imagine? Going the wrong way home? He got out of his car and stood on a bridge. He prayed to God and agreed that he would sell everything he owned and commit his entire life to helping the street children."

What? Had I heard that correctly? Give everything away? What on earth for? That made no sense. Why would a person do that? I could understand that a rich man would want to give some of his money away. That is generous. But all of it? What was the point of that? If he gave everything away, what would happen when it was all gone?

Would he not become poor again just like the rest of us? Why would someone who had lived in poverty like me, who had escaped it, put himself and his family at such incredible risk to possibly end up poor again—and all for helping children he did not know?

"And so—"

"Wait," I interrupted. It is wrong to interrupt someone. I knew this. But I simply had to understand. Why in the world would a man do something like this? "Did he actually sell everything?" I asked.

My uncle smiled. I loved his smile. You can always tell when you are loved. And his genuine smile gave me such assurance. "He sold every last thing he owned."

I closed my eyes for a moment, trying to understand. This story was getting stranger and yet more compelling all the time. This made no sense. None whatsoever.

"Why?" I whispered. It was all I could manage.

My uncle smiled again as he continued. "He went to the streets and rescued children. He gave them a bed to sleep in. He built classrooms for them. He gave them three meals a day."

Three? Three meals a day for orphans and street children? This was all too much for me. A bed to sleep in. School. Food.

Could a place like this actually exist?

And if it did, why would he bring children he never knew into his home?

"He started in the city of Eldoret. But he outgrew his home there. So, he built a new home in Ndalani for all of his children."

His children? How was it that they were *his* children? Would this actually mean …?

This far surpassed everything my uncle told us about food, clothing, schooling, shelter, and on and on and on. It was already incredible. Far more than any child I knew could hope for. But more than this, these children were actually becoming his children, and that meant that he—

"He becomes their father. And his wonderful wife, Esther—oh, wait until I start talking about her, I could go on and on. She is right from heaven. And she becomes their mother."

I felt a jolt of electricity shoot through my body. Could this be possible? A father and a mother again? It felt so real it was as if I could reach out my hand and touch them right in the hut.

But then it suddenly became unclear why my uncle was telling us this. What good is it to show the palace to peasants? Peasants have no chance of entering. The palace only serves to further reinforce the difference between the rich and the poor in their minds.

Why tell us about a heaven I could not reach?

My uncle must have seen a look in my eyes or read something in my body language that indicated my worry and disappointment in knowing about this place and not being able to go. He leaned forward. He raised both hands, palm out, the way Kenyans do when they are trying to make a point.

"And the children go there for free," he said. "Nobody pays any money to go."

My mouth opened. I was too shocked to breathe.

"And that is not all," my uncle said. "There is something even better."

Better? How could any of this become better? The question was no longer whether Mully Children's Family was reality or fiction. My uncle's compassion convinced me the place was real. But now I wondered if this place would become real for me. I wondered if this might be the way for me to become a doctor. I was never going to be able to pay for it on my own. But perhaps this man might be interested in helping me. Perhaps he would be able to—

"I have spoken to Mr. Mulli," he said. He shrugged his shoulders the way humble people do when they want to ensure that what they are doing is not because of themselves. "I have made some enquiries."

I heard the pulse in my ears. I took in a breath. That impossible distance between me being a hungry girl in a hut and me serving as a doctor to the poor suddenly did not seem very great at all. In fact, it seemed like the impossible had become nothing. I gazed into my uncle's compassionate eyes.

"I asked Mr. Mulli if the two of you could come to his home. If he would be willing to take you in as his children. To give you a future. A hope. A love that would fill your hearts with the love only a father can give. And you know what he said?"

I had done nothing to earn this. I had nothing to offer Mr. Mulli. And the strange thing was, he seemed to be okay with that.

"Charles Mulli said yes."

My eyes lit up. Zemira was the first to jump. She had strong legs. She jumped well. We cheered as we wrapped our arms around our uncle and hugged him. Really hugged him. We squeezed him so hard.

My grandparents hugged all of us. It felt good to smile again.

"We leave tomorrow," my uncle said.

So quick. I turned to my grandparents. Their assurance spoke from their hearts through their eyes.

"So I will let you pack and have supper. I will come to get you early in the morning. Is that all right?"

As a matter of fact, it was.

Everything was becoming all right.

He smiled like it was no big deal. He was about to leave for the door when I stopped him.

"Uncle Raza?" I asked. He turned. Everything about him resonated with me. Yes, I was going to get a new father. But I had him as an uncle. And when someone loves you who is not your parent or your grandparent, you feel a different kind of comfort, a different kind of connection that comes when someone doesn't have to go out of their way to help you but does.

"Thank you," I said. Zemira nodded in agreement. If I was shy, she was even shyer.

He shrugged his shoulders. I think he winked. "That is not a problem."

"I really love you," I said.

In that brief moment, I knew I had touched him. "I love you too." Then he smiled. "Sleep well!"

He left. I watched him walk down the path until he was out of sight. A quiet man. Doing anything he could to serve those around him. I closed the door. We began to get our things together.

Suddenly, I felt that a whole new future lay ahead of me.

CHAPTER
seven

Packing when you are rich takes a long while. Packing when you are poor takes only a moment. All of my possessions fit in one bag, and a small one at that. I tossed in my only extra shirt, and a skirt, a pair of shorts, and old flip-flops that I kept only in case I lost my other pair. I could not really imagine wearing the old ones, though. I would sooner have gone barefoot. Nothing I owned was of much value to me. You cannot become attached to what you do not have.

We sat down. Grandfather prayed. He thanked God for the time he and Grandmother could share with us. He asked God to guide us as we moved on from here. I remember him thanking God for the food we were going to receive at MCF—something he himself was not able to provide, at least not to the extent he would have wanted. His faith was a mystery to me. He trusted God. Did not question Him. Did not become angry with Him. Somehow, he believed God was in control. In the midst of his rank poverty, he was a wealthy man of faith.

I saw relief and sadness in my grandparents' faces. On the one hand, they knew that Zemira and I had a chance at having a future—something they felt a burden to provide yet had no chance of fulfilling. On the other hand, they would not see us nearly as often, and we felt the hurt that separation invariably brings. Umer in Nyanza Province is a long way from Ndalani. It's even longer for people who have to pay what they cannot afford in order to travel there. I did not expect to see them except perhaps once a year at Christmas. I admired them for being happy for us to have what they never did.

As I went to bed that night I prayed to God. I was taught how to pray when I was younger, but I never did so with passion. I prayed because I was supposed to, because that is what good people do. I felt the passion in my grandparents whenever they prayed, and I wanted that too. That evening my prayer felt different.

Thank You, God, for this opportunity to go to Mully Children's Family. I do not understand why things have happened the way they have. But I trust You that somehow You have a good purpose for everything that has happened. I am so happy that I get to go … But, God, I am afraid. I am a shy girl. I am so quiet. I do not speak much, and this might make it difficult for me. Please help me to do well at Mully Children's Family. To study hard so that I can be used by You to help people get well. Help me to make friends. Help me, Lord. I am so grateful. Yet I feel so nervous. You are with me. You are with me.

You are with me.

• • •

Even when I thought the bus was as full as it could be, we would stop yet again and still more people would get on. I sat crammed between Uncle Raza and Zemira in a seat made for two. The bus bounced so hard when we hit major potholes that it sounded like the bottom had fallen out altogether. Zemira and I giggled every time we jolted in our seats.

I watched as the forests gave way to crowded streets. Whenever we slowed down or stopped, street vendors hurried up to the vehicle and tapped on the windows with their fruits and vegetables. We changed buses in the crowded station in Nairobi. I saw many buses and *matatus* coming and going in every direction. A *matatu* is a passenger van designed for about 8 to 12 people, but often the *matatus* were crammed with up to double the allowable passengers. It was not uncommon to see people standing on the back bumper as it drove down the road; however safe or unsafe that might have been, it looked like a lot of fun.

The whole bus station in Nairobi was complete chaos. Buses and *matatus* everywhere. Crowds pushing in every direction. How anyone could find their way around or make sense of the maze was a mystery to me. And yet somehow it all seemed to work together as if it had been planned that way. We boarded a bus headed from Nairobi south to the town of Sophia. We made one last change there, this time from a bus to an overcrowded *matatu*.

The winding and bumpy country road from Sophia to Ndalani felt different from the other roads. The hustle and bustle stopped. Everything became quieter. It felt as if I could breathe in a way you could not in other places I had known. It was as if the land allowed you to let go of your burdens, and you could just be free and take in the environment for all it offered. I saw people carrying water in jugs on their heads. A young boy corralled his small herd of sheep and one cow from the middle of the road off to the side to let us through. He waved as we passed, a bright smile on his face. A woman in a long red skirt and a white shirt, wearing a bright head covering of many colours, worked in a field planting her crop. Everything around me felt peaceful and relaxed. I wished I could relax, too. Instead I felt a combination of excitement and apprehension over my new future. My new life.

My new home.

I wondered how Zemira and I would fit in with our new surroundings. About whether the other children would like us. About whether we would meet the expectations, and what those expectations were, exactly.

I wondered about all the things children wonder about on their first day of school.

The bus slowed down. My heart sped up. I glanced out the window. To my right I saw a sign with black lettering on a simple white board, bordered by a white metal frame and hammered into the ground. This is what it said:

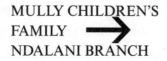

MULLY CHILDREN'S
FAMILY
NDALANI BRANCH

There was nothing fancy about this sign. Nothing about it that would draw your attention. If you weren't looking for it, you would drive right past it. This humble sign gave me the impression that a place as incredible as Uncle Raza made it out to be could also be the kind of place where a shy girl like me could fit in just fine.

The bus stopped at the sign. My uncle stood. Zemira and I picked up our bags and followed him down the aisle past the other passengers. I stepped down the stairs. My foot touched the ground.

This was it. For the first time. On MCF property.

We walked down a road that led towards a gate. The air smelled clean. Quite different from the fumes of all the vehicles in Nairobi. I felt a gust of wind blow across me as I looked up to my left. Far in the distance I saw large brown mountains. Their size amazed me, causing me to gaze with wonder. It surprised me to see only a few trees on them. I had not seen mountains before, so I could not compare what I was seeing to other mountains. Strange how seeing something for the first time can leave the impression that it does not look the way it should. More than the trees though, one large rock in particular at the top caught my attention. It sat so close to the edge that I thought it might slide off at any moment and come rolling down.

Lower down, beside me to the left, I saw a large football field. Many children played on the field, and still more stood on the sidelines watching. That sight alone told me a lot. Children having the freedom to play meant they had the energy to play and the comfort that they did not need to worry about their basic needs.

A little farther up, on the right, I saw a large field full of green crops. This, too, surprised me because from Sophia to Ndalani I had not seen many green crops. The landscape up to this point had been covered in a similar dry brown—as if someone had taken a big brush and painted the fields the same colour. But here the area looked different. Healthier. Greener.

We came to a security gate, where a friendly-looking elderly man wearing an old suit jacket and trousers stood and smiled at us. He waved as he approached us, walking with a limp. He shook hands and spoke with my uncle. It seemed to me they knew each other well because they talked and joked the way friends do. My uncle turned and introduced us to him.

The man smiled, excited to see us.

"Your first time here?" he asked. We nodded. "Very good. You are most welcome. Most welcome!"

That meant a lot to me. There is something encouraging about older people who take notice of young children who do not belong to them.

He pushed down on one end of the bar, which caused the end of the bar on the other side of a swivel to lift, making it possible for us to pass through. He waved at us and I waved back, noticing that he felt an incomparable joy in letting us enter this place.

The road curved to the right. To my left, I saw so many children that it amazed me how a group this large could be part of one family. How does someone organize all of this? How did all these children come to be here? Some carried books, others held wash basins in their hands, still others skipped together over a wooden bridge.

I heard the faint sound of singing in the background. I stopped to make sure I heard correctly. I should have kept going. I should have followed right behind my uncle. It is not polite to make people wait, especially considering the incredible place I was being introduced to. But the music so touched me that I had to stop. I had grown up singing with my grandparents; I had also heard it in church. But this felt different. This captivated me. It expressed something that far exceeded anything I had experienced before. I could not make out the words, but the tone and the spirit of joy reached right into my heart, giving me a sense of peace.

It made me wonder if music could have that effect on others or if I was the only one who felt that way.

The children all around me ran with energy and bright smiles. I loved hearing them laugh. I smiled as well. Then I began to laugh too. Their happiness was contagious.

I caught a glimpse of two large stone buildings with bright red roofs in the distance. In front of them grew a flash of beautiful red and blue flowers.

As I watched the children hurry past me, I suddenly sensed something out of the ordinary, but I could not explain what it was. Sometimes things are clear to your subconscious and it tries to send you a message, but for some reason it does not get through. There was more going on here than I was able to tell. I was seeing something I knew to be unique, almost impossible. It was there. Right in front of my eyes. Still, I could not define what made me feel that I was seeing something I had never seen before.

What was it?

As we walked farther, I saw many small homes made of metal siding and metal roofs. I had seen homes like this in Ndalani and other places. With Grandfather and Grandmother we only ever had grass roofs and mud walls, so these types of houses told me that the people here were not poor. They were not starving. If you can afford good materials for your house, you can probably afford good food for your stomach.

I saw lights through the windows of the houses. I had electricity in Nairobi when I was with my father, but not with my grandparents. I wondered how someone could afford electricity for all these people.

I smelled ugali and beans cooking. I took in the aroma and wished that maybe, just maybe, there would be some for us. Zemira smelled it too and turned to me with a big smile on her face. I tried to remember the last time we could eat until we were full.

It all seemed like it wasn't real. How could it be? MCF felt like a village unto itself that stretched on and on and on, without end, without restriction. A place where I could eat and sleep and have friends and go to school.

A place to have a family again.

MCF was a dreamland.

My uncle led us up a path to his home. He opened the blue wooden door. I expected to step on a dirt floor. Instead, I stepped onto concrete.

"Welcome," he said as we walked in. I saw his bed, a table, and chairs. "I am so glad that you are here." He gave us a hug. "What do you think so far of what Mr. Mulli has done?"

"Can I really say?" I replied. I was speechless. I could not even imagine a place like this in my mind, let alone explain what it was like to experience it in real life. "It is very good," I said. "And amazing."

"Do we get to play games here?" Zemira asked as we sat down at the table.

He laughed. "Yes," my uncle replied. "You will play many, many games here."

"Really?!"

"Really."

"What about jump rope?"

"Lots of jump rope," Uncle Raza said.

"And what about hide-and-seek?"

"Definitely. And even football."

"Football? I don't know how to play football."

"You don't?"

Zemira shook her head.

"You will learn. I promise you."

My uncle made us beans and ugali. He scooped in an entire plateful for each of us. We sat down at his little table, and he folded his hands. We were supposed to pray too. That meant we needed to close our eyes. But it was hard to. Zemira and I could only stare at our food. This meal alone would have lasted us three days back home.

My uncle prayed.

"Thank You, God, for bringing us here safely. Thank You for Hannah and Zemira. Thank You for providing for them to be here at Mully Children's Family. We thank You, Lord, so much for this supper. Please bless this food. And Father, we ask that You would intervene in the lives of those who have nothing to eat. Amen."

As we ate, Uncle Raza talked to us about MCF. He told us about the opportunities for education. About rescue ministries in the slums. About MCF's mission tours to other cities and countries. He explained about choirs we could join, even beginners like me. He also explained that MCF was a place where miracles happened. Many, many miracles. With every story he told and every aspect of MCF he shared, I fell more and more in love with all that was happening.

I felt the way people feel when they are at the beginning of a great adventure.

My uncle was about to tell us more about MCF when we heard a knock at the door.

"Welcome," my uncle said as he stood up. The door opened. A young boy slightly out of breath and beaming with excitement could hardly contain himself. His eyes lit up with joy.

"We are all asked to go to the devotion area," he said. "Daddy Mulli wants to meet with us."

CHAPTER
eight

We stepped onto a narrow wooden bridge spanning a shallow dry creek. It squeaked as we crossed over to the other side. We walked up a pathway, and to my left I caught a glimpse of a concrete structure similar in size to a small shed but not quite as tall. I saw the words *Jacob's Well* printed on it in black ink.

As we continued up the pathway, a sudden sea of children passed in front of me. The sheer number of children amazed me. I had seen groups of children before. Crowds even. Like at school. But not like this.

That feeling came back to me. There was something entirely different about these children. Some of the children laughed with their friends— genuine deep laughs that expressed a joy I wanted to know. They hung on to each other as if to keep themselves from falling over from laughter. Others ran as fast as they could, racing and cheering each other on as they hurried to get to the front. Still others sang beautiful African melodies that enveloped me. Captivated me. Their music reached inside me and calmed me in a way I had never known.

We got caught up with the crowd, and I sensed a rush of excitement as we joined in. It felt like being on a river raft and then suddenly catching the current as it races along. While I watched this happening, something about it seemed altogether different to me. I felt the similar feeling I had earlier. I knew in my heart that it was something obvious, but for the life of me I could not determine what was so different. We walked with the crowd and got pushed along to the devotional area.

This was just a big crowd, wasn't it? It was just more of what I had seen before, just like the groups of people wandering around the bus station and on the busy streets.

Or was it?

As we approached the devotional area, my uncle started leading us towards the front, but I stopped at the side, near the back, so as not to draw any attention to myself. My uncle noticed my apprehension and joined Zemira and me. We sat down on one of the many rows of rickety old wooden benches. I put my feet down on the mud floor. Above me I saw a sheet metal roof. There were no walls. I wondered if there was a symbolic significance to that.

My uncle sat between Zemira and me. He put his arms around us and gave us a hug. That felt better. So many people to meet and such a new place to discover all at once. And as odd as it might have seemed, I had the strangest feeling that I had been there before.

How could something so new to me feel like home?

Younger children sat at the front, older children at the back near the kitchen. I smelled the lingering aroma of the ugali and beans that the children had for their supper as well. They wore clean clothes—some looking like they had come from overseas. Friends talked with each other. And again my mind told me that there was something completely out of the ordinary here, and still I could not determine what it was. It felt as if someone was showing me the answer to a test question and I was not able to understand it. I looked at their smiles. Their eyes. Their laughter. The way the older children took the younger children by the hand and brought them to devotions. I looked closer at their faces—

And that's when it finally clicked for me. Yes, there were many children. Yes, they were of different ages. Yes, they were getting along as if they were the really big family they claimed to be.

But there was one thing that was completely different about this group than any other group I had ever been a part of before.

These children came from different tribes.

A wave of revelation swept over me. I was surprised. Curious. But mostly, I was in awe. Kenya has 42 tribes. Each of these 42 tribes fall into three ethnic groups—Bantus, Cushites, and Nilotes. Each tribe has their own customs, their own culture, and their own language. While the official languages of Kenya are Swahili and English, each tribe also has their tribal language. The vast majority of marriages are between people of the same tribe.

Me, I am a Luo. We are one of the largest tribes in Kenya. There are Kikuyu, Luhya, Kalenjin, Kamba, Kisil, Meru, Mijikenda, Maasai, and many others. The Maasai are the hunters. You might have heard of them. They are the ones who wear red. They can jump very high, and this helps them see animals far away while hunting. The Kalenjin tribe produces the runners. Have you ever seen Kenyan marathon runners? Those are mostly Kalenjin. It amazes me how one tribe in our country of Kenya can so dominate the world of international long-distance running. You can often determine a person's tribe by their last name. *Mulli*, for example, is a Kamba name.

As I looked around I saw children from many tribes. This was unique. In other parts of the world there are many different races of people living in the same area. People of European, Asian, and African descent might all live on the same street in some countries. But in Kenya, the tribes tend to stay in their own area. And tribes always stick together. People from outside Africa may not be able to recognize the differences. But when you are from Africa, or when you are here for a long while, you can see certain, sometimes barely noticeable, features that distinguish one tribe from another.

Why would a man from one tribe reach out to so many other tribes? Wouldn't he want to help children from his own tribe? How did all these tribes come together, behaving as if they were one? Mixing so many tribes together in a family was just not done in Kenya.

Yet here we were.

I leaned back, hoping not to be noticed, hoping to just blend in. Even though I had received the best welcome I could have wanted, I wondered deep down in my heart if I would fit into such a large family. I glanced down at Zemira. Without her saying anything, without even having to look into her eyes, I could tell from the way she sat that she was relaxed. I felt good to know that she felt welcome.

Children around me stopped talking. In that split second I sensed they were looking at me. This was the big test. What kind of family was this really? Was I in or out?

I found the courage to look at them. I am not entirely sure why I did. It would have been easier for me to take comfort in looking at the floor, to mind my own business and be shy.

But in their eyes, I saw something I had not seen before.

I saw their acceptance.

They smiled at me. "Welcome," a young girl said. The others followed. They waved at me like I was a friend they had not seen in a long time. There are people who welcome you with their mouths. And then there are people who welcome you with their heart. These children really loved me.

How was that possible, exactly? How could someone love me without knowing me? It was a mystery. But one that felt good. A moment ago they were strangers. Now, they were my siblings.

A girl a few years older than me stood and walked to the front. She turned and faced us. Everyone became quiet. "*Bwana asa fiwa*," she said, which means "Praise the Lord."

Everyone replied, "Amen." It was such a cool reply, all the children responding at the same time.

"*Bwana asa fiwa*," she said again, louder this time.

"Amen!" everyone shouted. It felt so loud under that metal roof. It gave me chills, despite the heat.

She began singing a song where she led with one part and then the entire group joined in on the next line. Back and forth it went.

Mambo sawasawa,	*Things are really better,*
Yesu akiwa enzini,	*When the Lord is on the throne,*
Mambo sawasawa.	*Things are really better.*

There may have been a couple of hundred children, but for me it sounded like thousands upon thousands of voices. I heard the higher soprano and alto voices of the girls. The lower tenor and bass voices of the boys. Adding my voice to theirs convinced me that we were part of something larger than ourselves. It was as if we were tapping into God Himself.

After the second song ended, the girl at the front sat down. Children began to clap in rhythm, like drumbeats in the African night. I glanced around, and, seeing everyone clapping, I joined in, not understanding what it meant.

Out of the corner of my eye, I saw a man stand up and walk down the middle aisle to the front. He was quiet. Unassuming. Gentle. He wore plain clothes. A pair of brown trousers. A button-down shirt. Glasses.

I was not able to explain why, but I focused my entire attention on him. I tried to see around the people in front of me to catch a better glimpse of him. I found my interest in him strange considering there was nothing unusual about his appearance, nothing that caused me to think he was anyone out of the ordinary. To me, he seemed like just a regular person.

So then why was I so convinced that this man was someone unlike anyone I had ever met before?

He smiled with a gentle smile. He waited patiently for the clapping to settle down and stop. And when it did, it all became so quiet. The man stretched out his arms and gave a thumbs-up with both hands.

"Ooo-aye," he said.

And with a loud, thunderous response that startled me, everyone shouted out, "Ooo-aye!"

"Very good!" the man at the front said. "I can see you are all very happy. Are you? Are you all really happy?"

"Yes!" they shouted again. It was so loud, it rang in my ears.

"Really? I mean, are you really happy in the Lord? I want to know."

"Yes!" they shouted again.

"Excellent. Then I think we can try again. Maybe even a little bit louder." He gave the thumbs-up again. "Ooo-aye."

I pushed my palms down on the bench and curled my fingers on the underside to stabilize myself. But it was of no use. I had never heard children this excited before.

"Ooo-aye!" they shouted back. It sent shivers down my back. I looked down at Zemira. At first she was shocked; then she smiled a huge grin.

My uncle did as well. He laughed so hard, I felt the bench shake.

"I am so happy to see you," the man at the front said. The children all became quiet again. Can you imagine? That many children, and all of them still? "I am so glad that we are together again," he said. "And I am so glad that we are together in the name of the Lord."

Even though I sat in a crowd of people, even though I was just one of so many children from all over Africa, I had the strangest feeling that this man spoke directly to me.

"There are many things we are learning. We are learning about things at school, and I want to tell you how proud I am of all of you. You are all doing very well. There are things we learn in our other activities. We learn how to play football, and I know we have many excellent football players here. We learn how to sing. I heard all of you singing, and I want you to know that you are all very good singers."

I hoped he would continue speaking for hours. There was something soothing behind his words, about the spirit with which he was speaking, that reached right into me. It was as if I could for a moment let down all of my defences with the assurance that only good would happen to my heart.

"But the most important thing we can learn is not just schooling or football or choir. These are all important, but there is something even more important."

We all focused on him. Not simply to look at him but to receive from him.

"The most important thing is to know the love of God in our hearts. We might think to ourselves—yes, I know the love of God. I know the verse 'For God so loved the world'—and this is good that we know the verse and other verses. But we need to ask God to make His love real to us. To have Him in our hearts. And once we turn our hearts to Him, His love will transform us moment by moment, and we can be healed of anything that is heavy on us."

I had never heard this before. Never heard that the love of God could reach inside me.

It is not possible. The love of God is something you must know in your head. That is all that is required.

No. He said that I could know God's love and that it would change me. All the pain I have in my heart …

Really? Maybe for others. But can you actually expect this is meant for you?

"This is available to each of us. God is near each of us. The Bible says, in the book of Zephaniah ... that is a strange name, isn't it? I do not think there is anyone here named Zephaniah, is there?"

The children laughed. I smiled. In that moment, the man showed himself to be both a confident leader and a happy child at heart.

"It says, 'The LORD your God is in your midst, a victorious warrior. He will exult over you with joy, He will be quiet in His love, He will rejoice over you with shouts of joy.'"

He spoke so quietly, so softly, yet it carried over the hundreds of children present, who were as silent as I was, hanging on his every word. Listening to him gave me the feeling he could talk for days on end. His words reached deep into my heart. *He will rejoice over you with shouts of joy.* Would God do that over me?

I studied the man at the front. Who was he exactly? What was he doing here? What was his purpose here?

I turned to my uncle and whispered, "Who is that?"

My uncle motioned with his head to the man at the front. "Him?"

"Yes. Who is that?"

My uncle leaned over to me. He smiled. "That, my dear niece, is Mr. Charles Mulli."

"Him?" I asked, searching the front. I glanced to the right of the stage, thinking that Mr. Mulli must have just arrived and sat down near where the man in the front stood.

My uncle pointed to the man speaking. I raised my eyebrows, then turned my head and looked at my uncle in disbelief. No way! But my uncle gave a slight nod. We both looked back at the man at the front.

Him? That quiet man at the front? How? How could such a humble man run such a large family? Would he not need to be a powerful man?

He did not look anything like what I expected.

He closed the evening off by praying and wishing everyone a wonderful night. He asked if there were any new children; Uncle Raza said yes, and then Mr. Mulli dismissed the group.

The three of us walked to the front as the other children left in the opposite direction. Part of me felt honoured to meet a person who had done such incredible things. Another part of me felt shy about him making time for us.

Did he not have more pressing things to do than to meet us? I saw how many children were here. I saw the fields. And if what I saw was only a fraction of what was here, then certainly there was so much more out there that needed his attention.

When he saw us, he gave us a big smile. That should not have had an impact on me; a smile is just a smile. But it did impact me. When he looked into my eyes, I felt like crying. He did not need to say anything. I stood in the complete assurance that he was thrilled to have us with him.

You cannot pretend to love someone. You either love them or you do not. And being with Charles Mulli for the first time—I knew he loved me.

"I am so glad to meet you," he said. "My name is Daddy Mulli. I would love to know your names."

Daddy. I played that word over and over in my mind.

Zemira leaned in to me to encourage me to go first. "I am Hannah," I said.

"Hannah. That is a very nice name. Like Hannah from the Bible, who believed God would answer her prayers."

He turned to Zemira. She looked down to the ground. Others would have mistaken this as shyness. It was that. But it was more. Sisters see things in each other that others do not. And I saw a little girl who, like me, was yearning for the affection of a father again. I knew it. She knew it. And most importantly, Daddy Mulli knew it. When he bent down to be at her level, I saw a man who was willing to reach out to a girl who was in desperate need of being loved.

"And I would like to know—what is the name of this beautiful young girl?"

Something in the way he said it caused Zemira to look up. She made eye contact with him. She smiled. "I am Zemira."

"Zemira. You see, another beautiful name. Now I need you to help me. What does the name *Zemira* mean? I am wondering; can you tell me?"

Zemira nodded. "It means 'song.'"

"You see?" And then he whispered. "Even with everything that has happened, God has brought you here. To your new home. And you will have a new song. How does that sound?"

Zemira nodded again, not breaking her gaze into his eyes.

He stood. "Very good. I am the father of all these children here. And you are welcome to call me Daddy Mulli. What do you think? How does that sound to you? I would like to know," he said with a laugh.

"Good," I said. "Thank you."

I said that so quiet, but I could tell he knew what this meant to me. To us. A new father. Who could have imagined this even a day before? Hearing that he wanted to be my daddy thrilled me. I felt as though a major piece of my life had been put back together. Like the roof of a house had been reinstalled. Like a ship that was once tossed to and fro, now sailing true and straight.

In all of this, he was not hurried. He was not looking to end the conversation so he could move on to his next appointment. He was content to speak with us. To be with us. To stay with us. There is something reassuring when an adult, especially a new father, has time for a child. We were brand new to him. And yet I felt I had known him my entire life. I felt like I was wanted.

I felt like I belonged.

"I want you to know that I love you very much. You are my daughters, and I am very proud to be your daddy."

I wanted to respond. I should have responded. But his words overwhelmed me so much that I could not reply, not even with another simple thank you. The tone of his voice, the look of compassion in his eyes, his gentle demeanour—it all made me feel that his words were true.

It was as if there was something coming from deep inside him that surrounded him, reached out, and enveloped me. I felt a complete calm come over me. The worry and all the anxieties of my heart slowed down and then disappeared altogether. I knew in that instant that I would remember this first encounter with him for the rest of my life. They say life comes down to moments. And for me, meeting Daddy Mulli was the moment for which I had been waiting a very long time.

What could I do in response to him accepting me into his family? What could I give him in return? Nothing, really. His grace was too much for me to comprehend. All I could do was accept it. And be amazed at how incredible all of this really was.

"I want you to know that you can come to me at any time. All right?"

We nodded. Although later his words would cause me to think about what he said.

He smiled. "Very good." Then he laughed with a deep laugh that filled the night air. There are laughs, and then there are Daddy Mulli laughs. Some laughs express joy, whereas others share joy. His was a laugh that gave you the sense you too could have what he had. A sense that whatever had managed to give him so much hope was also something that could be shared with you.

His laugh made us want to laugh too. And so Zemira and I laughed as hard as I could remember.

It felt good to smile. It felt good to know that there was enough hope for the future to make laughter possible.

"I will leave you with your wonderful uncle. He is a very good man. And he will help you to get settled in. How does that sound?"

It sounded like I was living a dream.

"It sounds good," I said. "Thank you."

Saying that did not seem like enough. When a man gives you more than you can possibly hope for, more than what your mind can even comprehend, you wish there was something you could say other than a simple thank you. A wave of guilt suddenly crashed over me. I felt a complete sense of being unworthy of what I was receiving. This whole thing felt like an unfair trade. He was giving me everything, and I had nothing to offer him in return except a faint expression of gratitude. It was not much at all.

But it was all my quiet heart could offer him.

"You are most welcome," he said. "Most welcome."

In that moment, it suddenly occurred to me we were no longer orphans.

I would learn so much in the coming time about how he communicated with people. How he said things. How he did things. How he believed things. How his gentle strength spread out around him like an invisible net, having an impact on those who had the privilege of knowing him. Especially those who, with broken hearts and disillusions about the future, could find him a representative of the gateway to discovering enduring peace and calm.

"Goodbye," he said. "And I will see you soon."

As he left, I wondered about his earlier line. *You can come to me at any time.* How was that going to be possible with so many children? Would there really be time for me to see him when I needed to? And yet, despite my thoughts, I had the unmistakable conviction that whenever I would need Daddy Mulli, he would be there for me.

At first glance, he *seemed* normal. Seemed like a regular person. Yet he was unlike anyone I had ever met, unlike anyone I had ever heard of. I could not put my finger on exactly what it was. I could not describe what made him so different. But even as a young child, I sensed that God was with him for this special mission.

He did not look like the boss of this place. He looked just like anyone else. Perhaps that is what made him unique. Perhaps greatness is best packaged with humility.

And if, in these few moments with him, I was able to experience such immediate unconditional acceptance, it made me wonder how I would be affected by my time with him at Mully Children's Family.

CHAPTER
nine

The sun sets quickly in Kenya. One moment, it is so bright that you cannot imagine anything but sunshine. Then comes the faintest hint of the light beginning to dim. It is so subtle that subconsciously you ask yourself if you are imagining it. The next thing you realize, it is pitch black. It is as if a great light switch gets turned off. And when evening arrives, I get to experience one of the greatest joys in all of Africa. I get to see the handiwork of God in the heavens above.

We use lights sparingly in Kenya. Part of the reason for this is that it costs a lot. Another reason is that we are used to the dark. We are used to not having manmade lights at night. There is something genuine and peaceful about living within what God has given us. For me it is a chance to see His unique nightly revelation of the stars.

What is it about stars that is so comforting? Is it because in their silence they seem to be saying something to us? Is it because during an otherwise dark time of day, stars give us hope that light exists beyond the troubles we face? Is it because the longer we look up at the stars, the more of them we see—reminding us that the longer we gaze at God, the more of Him we see?

I held Zemira's hand under the beautiful starry sky. We had said goodnight to Uncle Raza and were about to begin our walk back to the dormitories. We both felt apprehension in each other. I hoped seeing the familiarity of the stars would give us both comfort.

"What do you think, Zemira? Do you think they look the same as at Grandma and Grandpa's?

Zemira scrunched her nose as she rested her head back to get a better look.

"I think so. But there seems to be more of them."

"Well, you know what stars mean."

She gripped my hand tighter. I squeezed back to let her know that everything would be all right. I crouched down and gave her a playful push with my shoulder. She turned her gaze from the sky and looked with trusting eyes at me.

"It means it is time to meet our new sisters." She kept her focus on me. "It's going to be all right," I whispered. "You'll see."

I walked with Zemira under the canopy of lights in the night sky. I hummed one of the songs we sung in the evening devotions. I swung Zemira's hand back and forth in rhythm.

We stopped at the door of her dormitory. I sensed her nervousness. Nothing was said. Nothing needed to be. *How will I be received? Will I be all right? Will I make friends?*

I gave her a hug. "This is going to be a great time."

"Promise?" she whispered.

"Promise."

She swallowed. I felt her hand slip out of mine as she walked to the door. I thought for sure she would go straight in, but she stopped and turned back. For the first time, we would not be sleeping under the same roof together. She had so many new sisters just waiting for her through that door. She knew it. I knew it. I smiled to encourage her. She walked to the door and was about to turn the handle when she decided to knock instead.

It was light tap, one I was sure no one inside could hear. But I was wrong. The door opened. A young child—the same height as Zemira—gave a playful point of her finger.

"Welcome! Are you our new sister?"

Zemira nodded. The child hugged her with such enthusiasm that it caught Zemira, and me, off guard. "Welcome!" the young girl said. A woman approached and bent down and gave her a hug as well. "Welcome here. You are Zemira? Come inside."

Zemira nodded as she entered. More girls came around her, introducing themselves, welcoming her as they led her into the large room. I saw her face light up—like it was a surprise birthday party for her. The door closed.

She didn't look back.

When I heard the door click shut, I turned and began walking to my dormitory. Having Zemira with me allowed me to focus on her getting off to a good start in her new setting. Now that she was gone, I wondered if I would have the same courage I had just offered her.

I reached the light blue wooden door of my dormitory. I checked to make sure it was the same one that was pointed out to me earlier. Instead of going right in, I waited. It seemed so much easier encouraging Zemira to go into her dorm. As I stood there, I tried to rehearse what to say or what to do. But that becomes difficult when you have no idea who, or what, to expect. The longer I waited, the harder it became. Some runners say that the moments just before the race starts can be the hardest. I could understand why.

Part of me wanted to retreat to my own little world. To sleep in a quiet room all alone where I could be by myself. That would be safer, wouldn't it? The other part of me wondered what it would be like to be in a family again. What would it be like to have people to talk with and a place to call home?

One thing I was sure of—I wasn't going to find out by standing alone in the evening chill. I glanced up at the stars, trying to draw hope, then put my hand on the metal door handle. Knock or go right in? I pushed down and opened the door.

I slid off my flip-flops and didn't think anyone noticed my arrival. Putting my bare feet on the cold concrete floor, I turned the corner and looked into the main room. I saw 12 bunk beds spaced out evenly in rows. White mosquito nets fastened to the ceiling draped over the beds down to the floor, giving the whole room an elegant, enchanted appearance. I felt like I was in a storybook.

Girls sat in their beds. Some read books. Some talked with each other. They all looked so at home. Each had their place. Their activity. Their sibling to talk to.

Every room has a certain feel to it. You walk in and, without hearing a word, you sense the mood of the people in it. Even though I had never been in this dormitory before, even though I had never met any of these girls, I had the strangest and most welcoming feeling that I had been here my entire life.

It felt like I was coming home.

My apprehension vanished without me realizing it. I became consumed with the awe I felt of this new place. I wanted to stay here forever.

One of the girls, I couldn't tell who, called out to me. "Hello," she said.

A group of girls near the front turned to see me. Strangers staring at me should have felt awkward. Normally, I would feel a lot riding on an initial impression like this. But I felt none of that awkwardness. All I heard was that simple hello, but I sensed so much more. The tone brought me such calm that I did not remember the storm raging just moments before. And hearing how kindly that simple hello was said gave me a window into a world of acceptance I had not known could exist until then.

When you are poor, you have nothing to impress people with. No education. No fancy clothes. No rich parents. No achievements. I had no reason for them to include me.

And yet, for some reason they stood up to welcome me.

The first one was a Kalenjin. She was tall. A runner for sure. The next one was short, full of life, and swaggered as she held out her hand to greet me. One by one, they smiled at me with big smiles that revealed their teeth. More important, they smiled with their eyes. The brightness that sparkled through the brown windows to their souls reached into me, washing away all my concerns. In such a short time, I felt so welcomed, making me wonder how that was possible.

They introduced themselves. All from different tribes. All living together as if from the same tribe. I did not immediately remember all of their names. It was a lot all at once, and I had never met this many people at one time before. I felt an instant connection with each of them. Like they had been where I had been.

The longer I looked into their eyes, the more sure I became that I was seeing something deeper. Something that was true to their difficult backgrounds yet at the same time revealed their bright hope. A hope I did not have.

I knew from that moment on I would always remember them. I would always cherish how they welcomed me, a stranger, into their family.

You never forget who loved you in life.

"Karibu, Hannah!" a girl said. *Karibu* is the Swahili word for welcome. She introduced herself as Adia, meaning "valuable gift." Adia served as the dorm captain and had a lot of energy.

"And over there is where you will sleep." Adia showed me a bunk in the middle of the room. She pointed to the lower bunk. I was grateful for that. The top bunk was taller than my head. It would be a long way to fall. And, as my feet reminded me, the floor was concrete.

Adia turned to the wall as if just then remembering she had forgotten to mention something. "There's a locker for your belongings over there," she said, pointing to a box the size of a suitcase. That would be no problem. With my few possessions, I would not be needing anything remotely so large.

We walked to the bunk bed. Adia lifted up the mosquito netting.

"And somewhere under all this mosquito netting is your bunkmate, Isabella."

A set of hands from the top bunk began pulling up the netting. A lot of netting needed to be pulled up. Both Adia and the girl on the top bunk started laughing. A face at the top bunk appeared. Adia introduced me.

"Isabella, this is Hannah, your new bunkmate."

The moment I saw Isabella I knew we would be best friends. I felt her joy the moment she smiled down at me. So full of life. So real. It was like we had been friends our whole lives.

Adia turned to leave, I thanked her, and she shrugged her shoulders in that way Kenyans do when they indicate they are more than happy to have helped you. I reached my hand up to shake Isabella's, but her idea was much better. She climbed down and gave me the biggest hug I had received in a long time. There are hugs, and then there are Isabella hugs. Hers was a real hug.

Without knowing why, I felt myself begin to tear up.

She looked to be the same age as me. Same height.

"Nice to meet you, Hannah," she said.

I hugged her back, trying hard to understand what I was feeling.

And then without any warning, she jumped into my bed. She pushed her back up against the frame where my feet would have gone, scrunched her knees up to her chin, raised her eyebrows, and motioned for me to sit down opposite her. I got onto the mattress. Wow! Did that ever feel good! A real bed again. One that was raised off the floor. It reminded me of the time I slept in a bed at my father's house. I had two sisters back then.

I adjusted myself on the bed. My bed. I felt the soft blanket underneath me. As I pushed my back up against the bunk bed I felt a pillow behind me. A bed, a mattress, a pillow, a blanket.

Everything was going well, until she said, "So, tell me your story."

It sounded like a simple request. I should have just been able to open my mouth, and my heart, and fill her in on what brought me there. But instead of speaking, I froze. Something in me wanted to share my story. I wanted her to know everything about me. My best joys. My deepest sorrows. My dreams of becoming a doctor. My love of singing. But in that moment, I felt reluctant. Like there was something preventing me from letting someone in to see the real me.

You can't share your heart.

Why not? I want to. She would understand me.

How? Have you seen her smile? It is so genuine and so deep. What does that tell you?

That she is a kind person.

No.

Sure it does.

No. It tells you that she has a good life. That she has everything together. She is not like you. None of the girls here are. They don't have the problems you have. If you share your heart, they will not understand.

I sat up on the bed, forced a smile, maintained eye contact—did all the things people do when they try to stall and shift the topic of conversation in a different direction. I decided to keep quiet. Sometimes it takes time to build trust.

At least that's what I told myself.

"I am glad to be here," I finally said, trying to find words until I could shift the topic. "This is an amazing place ... Daddy Mulli is a really amazing man."

"He is. And to think, he was once poor and had to beg for food."

I nodded, hoping that by doing so I would not divulge that I used to have to do the same.

"So," Isabella continued, "I would love to know about your life."

Her quizzical expression and genuine love were evidence enough that all she wanted was to make me feel welcome. But what if I did tell her everything and she did not understand? Or worse, what if, after I opened the deepest recesses of my mind to her, she was not as interested as I hoped she would be?

"Thank you," I said. "I am happy to be here. I am sure you are, too?"

She understood my apprehension. She did not make a big deal of it. Did not take offence. Did not make the mistake of forcing me to go somewhere I was not ready to go. Instead, in her calm, gentle way she just moved on to help me out, knowing I would share when I was ready.

But deep down inside, I wondered what it would take for me to get to that place.

"Yes," Isabella said. "We have much to be thankful for. And to think of what Daddy Mulli had." She spoke quieter, as if doing so would help her understand the question she had on her mind. "I sometimes wonder, why would someone who earned all that money give it all away to help children he did not even know?"

It was strange to think that the bed I was sitting on would not be there, and I would not be there, if Daddy Mulli had preferred his wealth to us.

"Why did he do it?" I asked.

Adia called out from the front of the room. "Evening prayers and lights out, everyone," she said.

Isabella reached out and touched my arm. I felt comfort in her simple gesture. As orphans, one of the many subtle yet powerful things that disappear from our lives is genuine touch. For me, it seemed like with each hug and each touch of affirmation I received at Mully Children's Family, part of me was reviving after being in a deep sleep. "Sleep good," she said as she crawled out of the lower bunk up to her top bunk. "Great to be together with you."

I let those words sink in. *Great to be together with you.* I don't think she realized how much those words meant to me. It was a brief comment, yet she spoke with a heartfelt tone, giving me the impression she was the kind of person who communicated from a kind and compassionate heart. It made me feel safe. It made me feel wanted. It made me feel that it was going to be possible to be connected in a family again. From that moment on, I always remembered that even the slightest, smallest words can have the most profound impact on someone.

We said our prayers. Got ready for bed. The lights were turned off.

I tucked myself in under the covers. I felt the warmth that came with having a blanket around me and a mattress underneath me. With my head resting on my pillow, I looked out through the window at the stars. As I gazed at them, I heard a choir practising in the distance. It sounded so beautiful. So amazing. It almost felt like it came from heaven itself. In all my young life I had not heard such genuine, deep, convincing, and loving music. It completely encompassed me.

All music reaches our ears. Some reaches as far as our minds. But only a select few songs reach our hearts. And the singing from the choir stirred something in me and reached even deeper than all the suffering I had ever felt. My hands tingled. I felt a wave of emotion begin to well up within me. The stinging around my eyes grew in intensity and then subsided as tears came out and ran down my cheeks. It seemed as if the music was no longer coming from outside but rather from within me, like it had completely consumed me.

I blinked to squish more water away. The brilliant stars came back into focus. Something about them made me think it was so incredible that I was now here after where I had been. I had been at the bottom, and now I had a new home.

Daddy Mulli must have felt a similar way at some point. An abandoned child who, while working his way up to become a rich person, must have, at some point, had his first night in a real place he could call home, and he must have felt the same way I did. And from there he had gone to incredible new heights. And then to give everything away. Astounding! I am sure people thought he was crazy. And yet, here I was, someone grateful that he had in fact done what he did. It made me wonder if God had that all planned for his life from the beginning.

And it also made me wonder what God might have planned for my life.

CHAPTER
ten

I woke the next morning to the gentle sound of Isabella whispering my name. Her compassionate tone assured me that I had nothing to worry about and everything to look forward to. Normally waking up meant the start of another day of wondering if there would be enough food, if there was any chance of a better future. Today was different. In that foggy moment when I switched from my dreams to the waking world, I wondered how I could feel such peace from someone I had only met the night before. There was something special in hearing my name from someone who cared.

In that moment before I opened my eyes, I noticed that I had been at real rest. Both my mind and body had relaxed. I had not felt this since my mother was alive. While it was a welcome relief to know it was possible for me to sleep in peace, it also made me wonder if I was coming to terms with the passing of my mother, father, and twin sister. Was it all right to sleep well after they were gone? Or was my rest a betrayal because I was no longer remembering them? Was it a sign I was forgetting them? Or was it a sign that after all these years I was starting the difficult process of healing?

I open my eyes and saw Isabella. She smiled, and again I wondered if we hadn't met somewhere before MCF. The connection was too strong, too undeniable, for this all to be chance. In a fraction of a second, in a blink of an eye, I saw the real Isabella inside those bright, vibrant pools of brown. It reminded me of looking into Leah's eyes when we used to wake up on the mud floor of our hut. Ever since I lost her, I had wondered if that part of me that felt true oneness with her would ever return. Seeing Isabella made me think this might be possible.

Isabella laughed.

"We have the whole day ahead of us," she said, grabbing my arm. "Let's go!"

I smiled. "All right. All right," I said, getting out of bed.

"Quick. You have to get changed," Isabella said, stretching out her arms. "You need to be given the grand tour."

"All right," I replied as I stood to my feet. I glanced around the room. Girls woke up and got their beds ready. I heard people talking outside. The smell of breakfast filled the air. I still tried to convince myself that this place was not wishful thinking. That it was real. Strange that I had been born and raised in Kenya, yet this place felt like a fairy tale. And I was in it.

I wondered what we were going to do. Would we go on a hike? Go exploring around this mysterious, fantastic property? Was it time for school—for learning together with my new brothers and sisters? Or perhaps it was time for breakfast.

"Time for chores," Isabella said.

Isabella made up her bed. I watched to learn how to do it. A small red Bible lay on her mattress. I saw her put it in a space between her mattress and her bunk bed frame.

She led me to the door. We put on our slippers and walked outside.

The sun gave a beautiful quiet light. It cast a haze over the trees, as if they too were just waking up. I saw children sweeping the ground with hand-held brooms made of twigs from trees. A girl in the distance carried a basket full of clothes. I smelled a wood fire and a breakfast of maize flour porridge cooking. A village coming to life.

"Here," Isabella said, giving me a broom. She bent down and began sweeping the twigs and leaves that had fallen to the ground. I copied her, wanting to make sure I was doing this the right way. "Today you will get to see MCF," she said with her unique smile. "You will love it."

"I heard singing last night," I said. "Who was that?"

"One of the MCF choirs."

"How many are there?"

"Four at least. New ones are starting all the time."

"How do they get new members?" I asked, checking again with Isabella's sweeping.

"Anyone can join a choir. There is a select choir of the best voices. That one goes on tour. Why do you ask?"

Because that was the best music ever. I would do anything, anything, to join that choir!

"Just curious," I said.

But she understood. Soulmates always do.

"We will watch a choir practice today. Then you can see first-hand what it is like. How does that sound?"

I smiled, nodded, and shrugged my shoulders to indicate I was good with that.

Deep down inside, I felt such a surge of energy that it made me wonder if my joy would grow even stronger when I saw the choir first-hand.

• • •

After we finished sweeping, we got ready for the day. We walked under the protection of trees to the devotional area, which doubled as the place where we would have our meals. We joined a line of children in front of the kitchen. Isabella picked a red plate out of a bucket. I took a blue one. I watched as someone scooped food onto each child's plate. There was more food on one plate than I was used to eating in a week. It came to my turn.

"*Habari!*" the cook said, meaning "how are you?" He looked closer. "You are new? Your first time?" I nodded. His face lit up. "Hey! Great. Welcome. Welcome. So glad you are here."

He had a shaved head, a strong build, and a wide smile. I am guessing he saw hundreds of children each day. And in spite of that, he picked out immediately that I was new.

I felt special not to be a face in the crowd.

I glanced around for Zemira. There were so many children. It was hard to pick her out.

He scooped out so much porridge that I had to hold my plate with two hands. I tried to tell myself I could eat all this for breakfast. That I didn't have to package it up to ration it out for the week. That there would be another meal at lunch, and then another meal at supper.

"*Asante sana*," I replied, meaning "thank you very much."

"*Karibu sana*," he replied, meaning "you are most welcome." He asked me my name. I told him. "You are most welcome, Hannah. Most welcome to MCF. We are your family. And we are so glad to have you. So glad."

I gave a quiet nod of my head. On the outside I am sure I seemed as shy as I felt. On the inside, I could not have felt more welcomed.

I followed Isabella to a spot under the roof. We sat on one of the rickety wood benches near where I sat the night before. She bowed her head and closed her eyes.

"Thank You, Father. Thank You. Thank You. Thank You. Thank You for giving us food."

She looked up and began eating. Her prayer was nothing out of the ordinary. Not for her. But it was for me. In that short moment, she demonstrated a connection to the Almighty I could only dream of. She was so confident, so grateful, and so sure of His existence. It was as if she could reach out and touch Him just as easily as she could touch the food in front of her. I wondered how she knew God so well.

I swallowed my first mouthful. I stared at all my food, trying to believe what I was seeing. I took another bite, then another. I resisted my mind's trained message telling me to stop eating. I had been programmed to eat small amounts. To make sure I would save food. Instead, I continued eating. I finished my plate. I glanced around again, looking for Zemira.

"Would you like some more?" Isabella asked.

I shook my head and felt something I had not felt in a very long time. I was full.

"Hello, Hannah!" a familiar voice said.

I turned to my left. I saw Zemira with a group of about ten girls who had all finished eating.

"Hello, Zemira! How are you? How was your night?"

She took a step towards me and then stopped as she noticed her group beginning to run towards the football field.

"Everything is great. I can't talk! I have to catch up to my friends—my sisters! Bye!"

And with that Zemira chased after her new-found siblings. I felt a sense of peace come over me. Knowing Zemira was all right took a weight off my shoulders I had not realized was there until it was gone.

We rinsed our plates under an outside tap and put them in a bucket where someone would wash them for us before the next meal. As we walked away, I paused to look out at the mountains in the distance. I became captured again by the rock that looked like it was about to fall down. It amazed me that it was still in its place. It seemed like a feat of nature to be hanging there so precariously. I felt like I could watch it for hours, waiting for it to fall.

"We call it Mulli Mountain," Isabella said, looking out at it with me. "And that piece that hangs on the edge—we call that Pride Rock."

"From the movie *The Lion King*," I said, remembering the animated film about a young lion named Simba, which takes place in Kenya. I recalled the part where Mustafa, the young lion's father, died, and how helpless Simba felt. In that moment, the sting of my father's passing gripped me as if it had just happened. That feeling of abandonment, of questioning, of being alone in the dark and unsure of which way is home came over me.

"Whenever I see Pride Rock, it reminds me of a verse in Psalms," she said. "I will lift up my eyes to the mountains; from where shall my help come? My help comes from the LORD, who made heaven and earth." Her voice trailed off, as if she too were remembering something from her past.

She whispered so quietly that at first I wondered if she was speaking at all. "Sometimes things happen in life that are so hard ..." She stopped. She held her breath a moment, then gathered courage to finish her thought. "Even the most incredible things on this earth, mountains for example, cannot help us. But God can help." I saw her lift her hand ever so gently to her eyes to wipe away a tear that had formed. "God can help."

By the shakiness of her words, I had the distinct impression that her past was at least as difficult as mine, and perhaps even more so.

She turned to me, her bright smile returning. "Let's go explore."

• • •

We walked near the dormitories and came to the concrete structure I had seen earlier with the words *Jacob's Well* written underneath. This time I also saw nicely stencilled handwriting that said *The power of prayer*.

"How did it get its name?" I asked.

"It is a miracle."

"This well?"

"Yes," Isabella said, leaning up against the wall. I stepped closer and touched the concrete, as if to convince myself it was actually there, that it was no mirage or trick. I wanted to believe that the miracle story I was about to hear was as real as the concrete I felt against my fingers.

"Daddy Mulli started rescuing children by bringing them into his home in Eldoret. But it became too crowded. So he began bringing children to a new home here in Ndalani. God showed him to come here."

"Showed him? How did God do that?"

Isabella smiled. "God has his ways. He talks to us."

Talks to us? God in heaven would actually do that?

For good people. Not you.

"He talks to all of us," she continued, as if she were stating the obvious. I nodded, though I did not know what she meant.

"He brought many children here. But the river water became undrinkable. And many of the children became sick. So Daddy talked to people about drilling holes for water. But there was no water to be found. Not in this entire area. And there was no money to bring the water in. It looked hopeless."

I imagined the desperation Daddy Mulli faced, to be responsible for so many children and not to be able to provide for them.

"So Daddy Mulli prayed. He prayed very hard and very long. And then, in the middle of the night, while Daddy prayed, God called him to stand up and to go outside. So Daddy and Mommy ran outside. They turned this way and that, following God's leading. And God told him to stop right here," Isabella said, pointing to the ground.

"How did he know to stop here?"

"He knew in his heart God had spoken to him," Isabella said.

This all seemed too incredible to me. God in heaven speaking to someone and telling them to go in the middle of the night to a place in a forest to find what everyone said wasn't there?

"They prayed right here and dedicated this place to God. The next day many of the MCF boys started digging. They dug for an entire day. But they found nothing. Not a drop of water. It looked like Daddy Mulli had made a mistake. No one wanted to say it to him, but they thought he might have heard wrong."

"Did he feel sad?"

"Daddy? No way. He was completely sure."

"So what did he do?"

"He told the workers to keep digging."

"Didn't they think it was pointless?"

"They did. But Daddy Mulli knew it was the right thing to do. They dug for another entire day. They were exhausted. Everyone was exhausted. And then, guess what?"

This doesn't happen, does it? God doesn't actually tell you where there is water, does He?

I watched her eyes. I touched the concrete again.

"All of a sudden," Isabella said, "water shot up. People came running from everywhere. Everyone shouted water, water, water!"

I stepped back in awe. Like I was on holy ground and I suddenly felt unfit to be standing on it. *The power of prayer.*

Isabella pumped the well. Water began to pour out. I held my hand out and felt the cool water pour over my fingers.

I wasn't sure what else the tour was going to include. But even if this was it, this was more than enough.

"Where did he get the name?" I whispered.

Isabella paused. I think she sensed that the story of the well was affecting me more than she initially assumed it would.

"From the Bible. Jesus came to Jacob's Well to take a break. He met a woman there."

I found that interesting. Perhaps He would meet me, too.

"Want to see the farms?" she asked.

• • •

Isabella walked me through the large farms on MCF property. French beans were the largest crop. She explained that we exported those overseas. MCF also grew cabbages, tomatoes, and many other vegetables. Much of the other food grown here was for the children. We toured the storage area where they kept all the food. Then, we came to the schools.

"These schools are a miracle, too," Isabella said.

Of course they were.

"At first the government would not issue us a school permit," she said.

"Why not?"

"They did not think street children or orphans would have any hope of succeeding."

"What did Daddy do?"

"He prayed. Then he visited the minister for education."

"That takes courage."

"Daddy is not one to take the word 'no' very easily. Especially when it comes to our care."

"What did the minister say?"

"He loved the idea. He was so enthusiastic. He overruled the lower person and issued the permit."

"It must have been a difficult first year, to go from no school to suddenly having to write exams."

"Not really. We got the number-one spot. Our school had the best grades."

I stopped. Impossible.

"In the Ndalani area?"

"Not just number one among the 11 schools in Ndalani. But we were number one in the 124 schools in the Yatta division. And also number one among 940 schools in the Machakos district."

She kept walking. But I stood still. Isabella laughed. "Come on. Let's go! There's lots more to see."

Whatever world this was, she was so comfortable in it that she had gotten used to it.

She walked me past the teacher residences. More miracle stories. Past the dormitories. More miracles. Past Thika River. More miracles.

Isabella looked out at the mango trees and told how much she loved the fruit. I bent down as I listened to her, touching the ground and looking at the soil. It seemed normal. Seemed like dirt you would find anywhere else. I glanced up and around me.

What was this place exactly?

I heard the clanging of a handbell. The ringing sound came closer, and I saw a young boy running through the area, shaking it.

"That's our cue," she said. "Time for devotions."

• • •

There are two major school buildings at MCF Ndalani. One for primary students—grades 1 to 7, which we call standard 1 to 7. And one building for secondary students, for grades 9 to 12, which we call form 1 to 4. Today, all 427 of us lined up in front of the secondary school. No one wore uniforms, but all the boys wore pants and all the girls wore skirts. I much preferred this dress code to wearing complete uniforms like at other schools. I have always wondered why children who did not have the fees to go to school should be forced to spend money they didn't have on uniforms they couldn't afford. Maybe Charles Mulli's own history with poverty made him decide to do things differently here.

One of the teachers came to the front. He greeted us. We greeted him back. He encouraged us by telling us that God loves us and we are important to Him. We should not be afraid of anything, because God fights for us. In the same way that David came out from the Israelites and beat Goliath, Jesus fights off our enemies and makes it possible for us to succeed through Him.

It all seemed so unassuming, so plain. Yet his words hit me with such conviction, much the same way as had the singing of the choir the night before and the miracle stories Isabella told me on our tour.

He closed in prayer. People bowed their heads and shut their eyes. I looked down at the ground. A slight flutter of wind rose around us. I felt the conviction that God could, in fact, beat down each and every obstacle I had to face. I felt as scared as those Israelites did. Going to school with brand new people and starting the path to becoming a doctor was no easy task. I could relate to those Israelites hearing the taunts of Goliath. But then I thought about Jacob's Well. I thought about Daddy praying so hard and so long. I remembered the water flowing over my hands, the water that wasn't supposed to be there.

The teacher said amen. That meant school was about to start. A shot of adrenalin raced through my body. I took in a deep breath to offset the nervousness and followed Isabella into class.

I trailed Isabella and a group of students through a brown door into our classroom. To the left on the wall I saw a row of chalkboards. In front of me I saw the teacher standing behind her desk. She wore long hair extensions, a bright red shirt, and an even brighter smile. Students walked to the right and found their spots to sit. The desks were made of wood and seated two people. I followed Isabella, our footsteps quiet on the concrete floor. She sat down at her desk and slid over to make room, tapping the wooden bench and smiling to indicate this spot was for me. I felt glad about that. I sat down.

"Welcome to class, everyone," the teacher said. She looked over at me and smiled. "We have a new student. I would like everyone to say a very big hello to Hannah." The class greeted me. "Welcome here, Hannah," she said. "We are so glad you are here."

"Thank you," I managed, feeling both the joy of being accepted by such a large group and the awkwardness of being at the centre of attention.

She began teaching a math lesson on positive and negative numbers. I followed as best I could. She demonstrated how to solve the problems on the chalkboard. And after more lecturing, she gave us a number of problems on the board to solve in our notebooks. The other students each took their one and only pencil—part of the policy of making sure that nothing went to waste—and began solving them.

I however had no idea what to do. I was lost.

You will never understand it. It is far too complicated for you.

I felt my pulse begin to quicken. This was the real test, wasn't it? Was I able to do as well as the other students?

Don't bother. You will fail. You will be sent down two, maybe three, grades. You will have to say goodbye to Isabella.

The teacher crouched down beside me.

"How is it going?" she whispered, having the wisdom teachers have when they know the vulnerable place students are in when they don't understand.

I shook my head ever so slightly. I stared down at the −6 written on my book. I was supposed to add 7 to it.

"No problem," she said gently. She wrote the numbers −10 to 0 on my notebook. And then continued up to 10. "When we add, we go to the right. When we subtract, we go to the left."

That made sense.

"So what is your starting point?" she asked.

I pointed at the −6.

"Exactly," she said. "And now if you are adding seven …"

I moved my finger seven spaces to the right. I came to 1. She waited until I said it out loud to her. I chose to whisper. No point in being loud, especially if you are wrong. "Minus six plus seven equals one."

"Brilliant," she whispered back.

In less than a minute she showed me where I was confused. All the other problems she gave us to do suddenly became clear to me. Easy if, in fact, anyone can ever truly say that about math. I felt good to understand, to move from all those minuses to the positive side of zero.

"Now you try the next ones."

I did the next problem while she watched. Minus five plus five equals zero. She nodded. I did the next one. Minus three minus three equals minus six. I finished and showed her my answer. She gave me a thumbs-up and winked.

I could do this.

• • •

Each class became an adventure in learning something new. The teacher taught in such an interesting way. She asked questions, giving us time to think through our responses. I sensed that she loved me, so it was fun to learn. The classes included Christian and religious education (CRE), English, social studies, math, science, and Swahili. Even with more than 40 students in the class, she was able to create an encouraging environment that inspired us to believe that anything was possible for those who believed. Her faith was a curious thing. Powerful and contagious.

Other students talked about their dreams of becoming pilots, teachers, engineers, and many other professions. As I listened to them it occurred to me that this was not wishful thinking. It was a concrete fact for them. As solid as Jacob's Well. They spoke as if they had already been to the future to see that their dreams had become a reality.

Their confidence amazed me. I felt it reach its way inside me. Just by being around them I sensed myself switching from a world of wishing to one of believing. In less than 24 hours of being on this property, I found that instead of just hoping I could become a doctor, I believed I could actually achieve it.

At both our morning and afternoon breaks I went outside and played with the other girls. We took turns at skipping rope. They taught me a lot of new combinations, evidence of their innate dancing ability. We swung the rope faster and faster to see who could stay on the longest. We laughed ourselves silly as we clapped faster and faster in rhythm with the swing of the rope.

We played hide-and-seek in a large open play area, so I had to find clever hiding spots. I hid in the bushes, around corners of the buildings, and sometimes even behind other people. I loved playing these games.

They helped me feel like a kid again.

• • •

Isabella and I walked out of our English class. It was our last class of the day, and I already wished for tomorrow so I could learn more.

"I have to see my drama teacher for a moment. I will meet you later at the dormitory," Isabella said.

I nodded as she ran off. I walked under the hot sun and crossed over the bridge and heard it squeak. I was about to turn left to go to the dormitory when I saw a woman emerging from a large stone building beside the kitchen. The way she looked at me made me think she already knew me.

"Hello," she said, as she approached.

"Hello," I replied. I walked closer to her, feeling an instant connection, but I was not able to understand exactly why.

She began to laugh, as if simply seeing me brought her joy. "You are Hannah, one of the new girls who has come?" she asked, stopping in front of me.

"Yes," I said, looking closer at her, trying to remember if I had seen her before. "I am sorry, but who are you?"

The woman smiled in a quiet, gentle way. The way she did that made me feel it was completely okay for me to be me. I felt her acceptance without having to prove anything to her. Somehow, in just those few first seconds, she was able to convey to me that I was unique, that I was special, and that I was loved. I felt the relaxation and relief that comes from being around someone who provides security. Like the way a burst of sunshine brightens what was previously a cloudy day, her presence alone dispelled any fears, doubts, and concerns I could have about being loved. It was as if she had wrapped her arms around me, making my heart feel so warm. I had not felt this since—it had been a long, long time.

I studied her eyes. They were so full of understanding and peace, coming from a deep pool of joy that filled her soul.

"I am Esther Mulli," she said. "I am your new mother."

CHAPTER
eleven

Esther Mulli stepped forward and hugged me with all the confidence that comes from a loving heart. I felt her arms around me. Felt the joy that comes from a mother. I let the moment wash over me. Having met Daddy last night, and now Mother today, it occurred to me I was no longer an orphan.

Ever since my parents died, my deepest desire was to be loved by someone without having to be connected by blood. They say blood is thicker than water. Nobody understood this better than a child like me who had lost her parents. I was loved by my stepmother, but then she too left my life. With both my parents gone, I wondered if someone would care about me. *Will I be loved again?* I had tried to shut that question off because I did not see any way of that being possible.

Until I met Daddy and Mommy Mulli.

She pulled back and looked into my eyes. It seemed to me she had that rare gift of understanding what was going on inside me without having to ask.

"You are most welcome here, Hannah," she said. I believed her.

"Thank you," I replied.

She waited with the patience mothers have when they know their children want to speak but need the assurance that comes with not being rushed. We waited in silence. I admired her, even for this brief, impactful moment. And it made we wonder about moments like these yet to come.

"You are a mother to so many children," I said. "I can't really imagine how you do it all."

She laughed. "It is a lot."

Mommy Mulli studied me, looking into my eyes. Her smile subsided. This time it was her turn to be silent. Then, she spoke. "It takes the power of God to do this. Me, I could not do this on my own. But I rely on God." She became quiet again. Comfortable with the silence.

How did she rely on God to do all this? How can you be a mother to so many children?

"Could I ask you a question?" she asked.

I nodded.

"What do you think it means to be a woman of God?" she asked.

Children in the distance ran to the tap and took turns gulping water. They shouted with laughter. Normally this would have been cause for distraction, but she kept her eyes on me. I didn't know the answer. And she perceived this in me.

"Would you like to know?"

I did. I suppose every girl looks for someone she respects to bring her through the rite of passage into understanding what it means to be a woman. Yet what she was indicating was something more, something deeper. Not just a woman. But a woman of God.

I wondered what she meant.

"Yes, Mrs. Mulli," I replied.

"All right." There was that trademark smile of hers. "And you can call me Mommy, okay? Is that okay?"

I nodded.

That would be more than okay with me.

• • •

The Thika River runs along the edge of the MCF Ndalani property. During drought years, the river becomes so empty you can play football in the riverbed. In normal years, though, MCF children swim each day in its cool waters to get a break from the hot sun. Today, at a small clearing near its bank, down from the chapel and eating area, it served as the place where Mommy would share her wisdom with a group of girls.

We sat down on benches made from planks of wood laid over tree stumps. I felt the cool breeze of the wind. I heard the sound of rushing river water. Birds chirped above me in the trees that gave us shade from the sun.

Isabella sat down beside me. Other girls gathered around us, talking and laughing. Mommy sat at the front. The moment she started speaking, everyone became quiet. She talked in a quiet voice. Compassionate people rarely need to shout.

"You are my daughters. And I love you. Each one of you was made by God, and you were made with a purpose. There are no accidents. Not with God. With God, there is only design. He knows you, and He has a plan for you. A special plan."

I thought about my time in church when I was younger, listening to sermons I did not understand. I wondered why I wasn't affected during those times. Here on the bank of the Thika I heard from Mommy about the God who loved me. And this same God had planned me with a purpose. Despite my past, I had an undeniable conviction that God would do something good with my life. In spite of all that had happened, this was a place where not only I would be loved, but also I could achieve what I had been created to do.

"A true woman is a woman who fears God," she said. "You might ask, why should I be scared of God? But when we say we fear God, we do not mean to be scared. To fear God means that you believe in God. That you trust in God. That you obey God. That may sound easy, but when there are many things around you that do not make sense, it is very easy to ask, 'Where are You, God?' And this is when you must trust God."

I thought about what it might have been like for Mommy when Daddy told her he would be giving away all their money to help rescue kids like me. I am sure she wondered where the money would come from to help all of us.

"You see the trees around you. They draw their strength from water through their roots. In the same way, we trust God to give us His strength into our lives to accomplish His purpose. We cannot say, 'Look what I did'; we can only say, 'Look at what God did through me.' But we have our responsibility too. Every woman of God should be hard working. And we should be hard working in His power. So I ask you—do you want God to live His life through you?"

Live His life through me? How would that work? I wasn't sure even how I worked, let alone how God was to be working through me.

"Be faithful in whatever duty you have. Sometimes people want bigger duties so that they feel more important. But God does not evaluate us on whether we are doing big things or small things. For Him, it is not a question of big or small but of faithful or unfaithful. Whether you are a mother to hundreds of children or you are sweeping the ground, in God's eyes there is no difference. If you are faithful in what you are called to do, you are a woman of God. God gives to each woman different tasks. It is not up to us to question why someone gets certain things and we get different things. Our God is a wise God. We should take from His hand what He gives us and be faithful with it. We should work under His eye. If we are in Christ, we already have His approval. So why should we worry?"

I felt the sincerity of her words. And it made me wonder what she meant when she said *in Christ*.

"You will find in life there are many distractions. Especially when you leave MCF." Those words hurt. I had just arrived. I could not imagine leaving MCF. I wondered if, in a way, I never would. Even if you move away, how to do leave your family?

"When you leave MCF, you will be in a world where you will have even more things around you. The busiest man ever was Jesus. And yet, Jesus took time to pray. With everything going on around Him, He prayed to God. I want each of you to know that women of God are women of prayer. Sometimes women say they are following God. Are they really? You just have to ask if they are praying women. That will tell you the real answer. Jesus said, 'When you pray, go into your inner room' and 'close your door.' The real quality of a woman is not simply what she does when she is seen but what she does when she is not seen."

As a quiet person, I sometimes felt pressure that I was not making the same impact louder people did. In listening to Mommy, I felt encouraged that whether I was talkative or quieter, the key was not so much our outward actions but our prayer time with God.

And it made me ask myself if I was a woman of prayer. I did pray. On occasion. But even when I did, I was not really sure how to pray.

"Remember the women who went to the tomb after the resurrection of Jesus from the dead. These women trusted in God. They were women of faith."

She cleared her throat, grinned, and adjusted her wide-brimmed hat. "And now I would like to speak to you about marriage."

That sparked everyone's interest. Some girls giggled. Others shifted in their seats. Mommy laughed. "I thought that would get your attention." We all laughed with her.

"There are many things to say about marriage, but let me emphasize this. When it comes to finding a husband, the key is to be patient. We should not be in a hurry to get married. There is no hurry, not with God. Pray to God that He would give you a good husband in His time.

"For those who have their faith in Jesus, we must remember that we are complete in Christ. Sometimes women look to marriage to give them purpose. But this is not correct. You are complete in Him. Then, when God in His perfect timing chooses to give you a husband, you are able to serve together. Some girls get married when they are young, even at 15 years old, and they drop out of school. Life is really hard for them because they cannot provide for their children. They haven't studied. If you have not finished your studies, you have not finished your skills. It will not be a happy marriage, because you don't have the resources to handle your kids or your marriage. At MCF, you are given the opportunities to learn and to work hard. Education and your training here are practical and will help you."

She paused as she looked out us. Her wisdom helped to solidify in our minds and our hearts the practical reality of what it meant to be women of God. I wondered if I had what it took to live it out. Prayer, trust in God, being complete in Christ. It seemed like a lot. Especially since it was the first time I was hearing this.

"And one last item," she said. "Remember to look after the younger girls. We should all be responsible not simply for ourselves but also for the younger girls around us. Remember, the more you serve, the closer you will grow to God. When we live for ourselves, we end up with nothing. But when we truly surrender and allow God to live in us so that we are serving others, we really discover what we were meant to do."

I thought about how Mommy had given up so much. She surrendered her life of wealth and comfort to serve us. I hoped I would have the same courage.

• • •

Isabella and I left the bank of the Thika and walked back up the hill to our dormitory.

"What do you think?" she asked.

I should have asked her first. Now I was on the hook to respond.

"She is a good example," I said. "She is a real woman of God. What do you think?"

"I agree. So, who are you going to marry?"

I pushed her and quickly looked behind me to see if anyone else had heard. "Quiet! You tell me, who are you going to marry?"

We made it to the top of the hill and turned right towards the dormitory. When we reached the door the other girls walked in, but I stopped and looked up at Pride Rock, sitting there so precariously, as if a finger from heaven was holding it up to keep it from sliding down. I thought about the challenge of being a woman of God. It seemed like such a lofty goal to aspire to. One I questioned whether I had it in me to accomplish. Part of me knew that the answer lay all around me. It was clear to Mommy. I sensed it was clear to Isabella, too. It felt like it was within arm's reach of me.

I don't know how to be a woman of God.

My eyes drifted down to the valley below. I saw the combination of mostly brown with some green areas. I glanced back up to the mountain.

I am not even sure of how to pray to You or how to do any of the other things Mommy talked about ... Can You show me how to become the way You want me to be? I don't know how. But I know that You can.

CHAPTER
twelve

I cannot imagine a better supper than eating *chapati* together with Isabella. This unleavened flatbread comes in the shape of a circle and fills your entire plate. It is a favourite of the kids at MCF. Like other simple things in life, it brings me great joy.

When it was my turn in the line, I held out my blue plate, and the same man smiled to me as he gave me a chapati. I sat down with Isabella on one of the benches, took a bite, and inhaled the warmth of the bread. Isabella and I discussed what we had learned from Mommy Esther. I saw so much of Mommy Esther in Isabella. Isabella had this joy in her. This calmness. This peace.

"So we have two fun things this evening," she said.

"Great! What are they?" I asked.

"First, we have our weekly Bible study after supper. Usually we have one of the teachers lead it, but for the next while we will have a guest teacher."

"Really? Who?"

"I am not sure. But this person is not from MCF. If I heard correctly, I don't think he is even from Kenya."

"Uganda?"

"I don't think so."

"Tanzania? Why would he come all the way here to us?"

"I think he might even be from farther than that."

"Why would someone do that?"

If you ever visit Ndalani, you will soon realize that we are really a long way from anywhere. I would not go so far as to say that we are in the middle of nowhere. But we are close. Those of us who have been rescued, however, know we are at the very centre of where we should be. Still, Nairobi is our capital. And it takes two buses at least to get to MCF.

Why would someone come all the way here when there were many other places to visit?

"And then ..." Isabella began, pausing for effect, or just to annoy me. I am not sure which.

"And then what?"

Isabella laughed. "Nothing. Just a surprise. You would not be interested."

"Isabella."

"Do you like surprises? I didn't think so."

"Isabella, tell me. What happens after Bible study?"

"Have you had enough chapati?" she asked.

"Don't change the subject."

"Which subject?"

"Isabella!"

"Hannah."

Isabella laughed again. This time uncontrollably. "Okay, okay. You want to know?"

"Yes."

"Are you sure?"

"Now you tell me!"

Isabella took in a number of breaths, trying to calm herself down. Then she looked back at me. "After Bible study today," she said, "you have your first choir practice."

• • •

As we walked up to the classroom, we said hello to one of our sisters, who was in the classroom next door, finishing her chore of washing the floor. She wrung out the rag one last time in the basin of water and cleaned the final stretch of concrete.

Just as we opened the door, Isabella commented on how much she liked my shirt. I thanked her. It was my favourite. A long sleeve white shirt with a seahorse and a starfish. We received clothing from supporters all over. And it made me wonder if the family who sent it to MCF had a daughter my age and if they lived on the coast somewhere in the world.

We entered our classroom. I saw a man arranging some of the desks into a circle. When he heard us enter he turned and smiled. He asked us our names. Then he told us how glad he was to see us. He was white. It made me curious about where he was from, so I asked him. He said Canada, and I wondered what life would be like in a far-off place like that.

I noticed a Bible on his desk. That was expected for a Bible study. But he also had a stack of other Bibles. That was new. At MCF we only had so many to go around, and we didn't all have our own Bibles.

Other students entered. We sat down together in a circle. He handed out small pocket Bibles to each of us. We opened in prayer. The moment we closed our eyes, I sensed a complete peace come over all of us. It seemed there were suddenly more people in the room. I felt like opening my eyes to see if it were in fact so but kept them shut instead. As I heard people taking their turns praying, I knew that this presence was more real in my heart than if I could see it with my eyes.

When we finished praying, we took turns introducing ourselves. He was interested in memorizing each of our names. I wonder if he learned that from Daddy Mulli. Isabella told me that Daddy Mulli knew every child's name at MCF.

We took turns reading from Psalm 1.

But his delight is in the law of the LORD,
And in His law he meditates day and night.
He will be like a tree firmly planted by streams of water,
Which yields its fruit in its season
And its leaf does not wither;
and in whatever he does, he prospers.

This passage comforted me about becoming a doctor. I felt the challenge of reaching that goal, and knowing God would plant me and prosper me helped ease the burden.

The man encouraged us to constantly live in God's presence and to take time each day to spend with God praying, just as this passage said.

The more I listened to what he said, the more it sounded similar to what Daddy and Mommy, our teachers, and our pastors taught us. Here was a person from the other side of the world who spoke with the same spirit as followers of Jesus in Africa.

He gave us one last encouragement from John 16:27. *For the Father Himself loves you.* I read the verse over and over again in my mind. The more I read it, the more I felt it speaking to me. What did it mean for God to love me? And was this something that I knew in my mind or something that I was convinced in my heart to be true?

When he announced that we would close in prayer, I was surprised the time had gone so quickly. As we left the classroom I turned back to him.

"Why did you journey all this way to be with us?" I asked.

He paused a moment. "God put it on my heart to come to MCF. And being here with each of you is simply amazing."

"Thank you," I said.

"Thank you for having me," he replied.

"See you later."

"See you," he said. "And be encouraged to follow God wherever He calls you."

• • •

After leaving Bible study, we walked to another classroom. We opened the door and saw two long rows of students in the middle of the room, facing the front. The girls stood in the front row, the boys at the back.

"Welcome!" Dickson Mulli said. He is the youngest child of Daddy and Mommy Mulli. As I would later discover, when I was around him, or any of the other biological children, I felt there was no difference between those that were born in or, like me, adopted in. We were one family. I admired him for making me feel this way.

I took my place in the soprano section. Isabella stood in the alto section. We opened in prayer. Then it was time to begin singing.

We started dancing to a rhythm. It felt so natural. So fun. The music got into my blood and became a part of me. We all moved together as if we were one. We shuffled our feet and swayed our hips and shoulders. Something inside of me came alive as I felt the rhythm in my body, mind, and heart.

My shyness left me. It vanished altogether. I became so full of life as I sang. I listened during the verses, but the chorus proved easy enough that I joined in with my siblings.

Wamilele, wamilele Mungu	*A God who is forever, forever*
Wa baraka ni nina	*One who blesses, who is he*
Ni Yesu.	*He is Jesus.*

The longer I sang, the more I felt something new happening inside me. I had sung before in many other places. But this was different. I remembered the feeling I had when my mother sang to me. This felt the same way. Perhaps even deeper.

The sound of the singing filled the room. I loved the clapping and the different rhythms and dances with each song. I felt myself swept away with the music. It could go on forever.

And then, just like the Bible study ended so quickly, Dickson announced that this would be our last song for the practice. How long had we been here? An hour? Two?

I sang with the joy that came to me with every song. I was about to close my eyes to feel more a part of the music when out of the corner of my eye I saw that another person had joined our choir. I turned my head to see who it was. All the boys in the back danced back and forth, so it was difficult to see who had joined in. When just the right combination of boys moved in the same direction I managed to catch a glimpse of the person. It was Daddy Mulli! He blended in well. I noticed his good rhythm. He moved and grooved just as cool as the boys, if not better. He saw me looking at him. He smiled.

Daddy could really dance.

We felt the feeling singers feel when they are in a family united by the bond that comes with making music. I felt like we were one, like something larger than ourselves held us together.

The song ended. I hoped it would not be seven long days before we would be together again. I loved the feeling that lingered in the room after we'd been singing so long. The atmosphere felt electric. Like there was a charge in the air around us.

The room began to empty out. I waited, wanting to take in every last moment, much the way some football fans stay right to the very end even after their team has left the field. I was about to go when I noticed Daddy speaking with Dickson. They finished their conversation, and Dickson with his classic smile thanked me for coming. Daddy Mulli turned to me.

"Hello, Hannah. How are you?"

"Hi, Daddy. I am fine."

"I am so glad you are in the choir. Did you enjoy it?"

"I loved it!"

"That is good. I am glad to hear that," he said. "Where are you going?"

"Back to my dormitory."

"Great. May I walk you back?"

I nodded. How cool would that be? Walking back under a starry sky with my dad.

We stepped outside and felt the coolness that comes when the heat of day disappears with the fast-setting sun. The stars above filled the night sky like a dazzling show. Daddy and I walked down the steps to the area where we had the school devotions earlier that morning. He had not said anything, had not given any words of wisdom, not yet, but somehow it felt like he had already communicated so much to me.

"How are you doing, Hannah?"

I am sure there were many other children around us going back and forth; there must have been. With a family this large, there is always lots going on. Yet in that moment I felt like he was the only other person in the world.

"I am fine," I said.

"I am glad to hear that. It has been a big change for you. From where you had been."

In that moment, I felt a struggle return within me. It was as if Daddy Mulli's presence allowed me to face the truth of my unwillingness to allow others to see me for who I was.

It will be all right. Tell him. Tell him the fears you have about sharing your heart.

No! No, don't do it. You don't want him to think you are strange.
He loves you.
He won't understand you.
He has been where you are. He will understand perfectly.
It's too risky. Don't share. Just keep everything locked up inside for now.
There will be time later.

"I am really glad to be here, Daddy," I managed. He knew there was more coming. There always was. He waited patiently in the silence for me to continue, his conscience clear of any need to hurry.

"And I am glad to have you here," he said with the patience and gentleness that came with encouraging those he loved towards healing.

We crossed the bridge. This was the halfway point back to the dorm.
You are almost there. Just thank him and go inside.
He cares. Sharing is crossing the bridge from fear to trust.
You are new here. You are different. You don't want to ruin anything.
For the Father Himself loves you.

We walked to the dormitory. I had all the security I needed to share what was on my heart. Still, my fear was a strange and unwelcome companion. In moments like this, it was an irrational means to protect something that was crying out for restoration.
Don't. Don't. Don't.

"Daddy?"

Daddy stopped. We were alone under the stars. In the distance, I heard my sisters in the dormitory getting ready for the night.

"Yes."

He waited. He waited for me. I can't describe how comforting it felt to know I did not have to rush, to know I did not have to pretend. I released my feeble grip on my life and opened up to him.

"I'm scared, Daddy," I finally said.

I felt relieved to have finally said it out loud. I felt the power of words. The power of taking a leap and converting the pain inside me into something that could be shared outside of me. Then I realized how terrifying admitting this was for me. What if he didn't care? What if I had taken this risk of revealing the secret place of my soul only to have it rejected, or, worse, what if it was met with indifference?

"I understand," he said.

His words reached into me, like a wave of warmth that brought peace to my troubled heart. I looked into his eyes for assurance as he continued. "Sometimes sharing about our lives can be difficult. We think no one else will know what life is like for us."

How did he know that? How did he know that this was precisely what I was feeling?

"I am so sad about all the people who have died in my life," I said.

My eyes welled up with tears. I breathed in, then wiped my face.

"This takes a lot of courage," he said. "I want to thank you for trusting me with your heart. Healing is a process. And through sharing we can overcome the pain in our lives."

I nodded.

"You can come to Mommy or to me anytime."

"Thank you, Daddy."

I felt such a relief to have this out in the open. Especially with him. He had started me on a course, a course that a few minutes before I was unwilling to journey on. Yet he knew I needed his listening ear. Something in him drew it out of me.

"Grief can overwhelm us," he said. "It can feel like there is no way out."

Even though it was pitch black outside, I felt I could see clearer, like a fog had lifted.

"Yet God is great," he continued. "He uses everything for His glory. And if we have faith in Him, we can trust that He loves us in our pain, in our heartache, and in all of our questions."

I felt the wind pick up. It blew against me and then seemed to swirl upwards. The leaves rustled. I saw the treetops begin to sway.

"Thank you, Daddy," I said. He smiled. I felt drops of rain begin to fall around us. They came down in soft, gentle rhythm, as if a great conductor was causing them to do that.

We wished each other a good evening. As I walked to my dormitory, I thought about what he had said. God loves us in our pain. It caused me to wonder why God would allow it in the first place. None of this made any sense to me as I opened the door.

But a conversation I was about to have would change all of that.

CHAPTER
thirteen

Rain poured down against the roof of our dormitory. I sat up in bed, feeling the comfort of the steady rhythm. I loved the sound of rain in the evening. The combination of the pattering sound from outside and being in a warm bed inside made me feel protected. I pushed my back against the bedframe, tucked my knees under my chin, and wrapped my arms around my legs.

I heard the other girls talking with each other in the beds next to me. I liked the feeling of having my sisters around me, discussing things. I felt like I was in a miniature concert. The rain kept the beat, and the hum of the girls around me added the lyrics.

"Hey you down there," a familiar voice above me said.

I grinned. It was involuntary.

"Hey you up there," I replied.

"Well, either you're coming up here or I'm coming down there. And seeing how you are all snuggled into place down there, I think I will drop in to see you. How does that sound?"

"Sounds like a good plan," I said.

Isabella climbed down and sat down across from me. She pulled her knees up under her chin, like me. We were mirror images of each other. Her complete love and acceptance of me was perfectly transmitted through the light in her eyes and the genuineness of her smile. I felt the acceptance that came with knowing there was nothing I needed to, or could, do to gain her approval. I hoped she felt the same way about me.

"I am glad you are here at MCF," she said.

"I am glad you are here, too."

"I remember when I first came here. It was so different from what I was used to."

I didn't want her to have to go back into her past. Partially because I didn't want her to remember whatever tragedy she had to endure. And partially because if she shared about her life, then maybe, just maybe, she would ask me again to share about my life. I did not want that. Some doors are better left closed. Some letters are better left unopened. And some thoughts are better left unvisited.

"It's all right; you don't—" I started and then cut myself short. I could listen to her, couldn't I? I found myself wanting to listen to her. I loved listening. And I loved her. And so I did the only thing I knew how to do in that moment. I shared my heart as openly as I possibly could without holding anything back.

Honesty builds the best bridges.

"I don't want you to have to say anything you don't want to, Isabella."

We could just avoid all of this, couldn't we? She did not have to relive her past, did she? We could just stop our minds from ever looking back. Just close the door on this. Lock it all up. Throw the key into the river and move on with life, pretending that none of what had occurred in our lives ever happened. That would work.

Wouldn't it?

"Do best friends pretend things didn't happen?"

She was right. Maybe my fears about revealing my past were not well grounded. Maybe hearing her story would help us both. It would help her share her heart and help me to know there is power in doing exactly what Daddy Mulli said. There is peace to be found in sharing with people who care.

The rain pounded with even more intensity. It came down so hard that it drowned out all the other conversations around me. All I heard was the rain's drumbeat and Isabella's still, small voice, which, despite how quietly she spoke, cut through all the heavy rainfall and cut through all my fears of hearing about of her past.

"Please," I said. "I would like to hear your story."

"I did not have an easy beginning," she said. "My father died when I was very young. I don't remember much about him. A few images really. That's all. There were six of us in the family. Six is a lot of children. If you have money, then six children are wonderful. But if you are poor, and especially if you are poor and don't have a father, then six children spell disaster for all of you."

I looked deep into the brown circles around her black pupils. Her eyes said so much. There was such honesty in them and something else I couldn't quite place.

"We lived with my mother. But she was not able to take care of us. She was not able to find work. Not good work, anyway. Not many people could in Kipsongo."

Kipsongo. I cringed when I heard that word. Of all the places in the world for children to exist, Kipsongo shares the rank among the worst places on the planet.

Kipsongo is a slum near the town of Kitale. It is near Uganda to the west, and north of Eldoret, where Daddy Mulli started bringing children into his home for the first time. Kipsongo came into existence when people from the warring Turkana and Pokot tribes in northern Kenya fled their homes because of drought and violence. They went to Kitale but were unwelcome. In a desperate measure to survive, they found refuge in a dumpsite. The people of Kitale nicknamed the dumpsite *Kipsongo*, which means "Place of the Dogs" or "Place of Hopelessness." It is an apt description. All unwanted people from Kitale end up there. People exist in tents made of sticks and garbage. Kipsongo is home to the poorest of the poor. It is a place of sickness, disease, crime, and anything else you can imagine.

It is an unthinkable place for my dear friend Isabella to have lived.

"We had no food, no proper clothing, no place to live, and no chance to go to school."

She conveyed the difficulty of her past through her eyes. Instead of the spark she normally had, I saw in her the depth of character that came with suffering. She did not need to use words to describe what all happened. I saw it. I felt it.

"I had to ask myself a question—Do I stay home where I have a roof over my head but no food, and so I will eventually starve, or do I go to the streets to find food but risk having no place to sleep? If you have to choose between sleeping in safety and possibly starving and living on the streets with greater risk, which do you pick?"

It hurt me that she had to go through this. Hurt me that she had to ask the kinds of questions no child should have to ask.

"The agony of not eating won out, and so I went to the streets. I ate out of garbage bins," she said. "You have to be smart about garbage. There is good garbage, and there is bad garbage. Bad garbage makes you sick. Good garbage is hard to find. But you learn over time to figure out what to eat and what not to eat. Of course, that becomes more difficult to hold to the more days you have gone without food. You would be surprised what you are prepared to eat when you have had nothing for a long time."

I wanted to erase that image from my mind. I did not want to think that my friend had to go through this. I suppose this is a common reaction. We want to protect those we love. We want them safe from all harm. Even to the extent of rewriting their past to make it more palatable. And yet hearing about her suffering built trust within me.

My instinctive reaction was to tense up, to not want this to be true. Yet the more she spoke, the more truth she shared, it revealed to me the healing that came with looking into her past, not with regret but with an understanding that from her suffering she had grown to become someone different. Someone stronger. Someone who did not need to shrink back from where she had come from.

"We also went to restaurants. You know the back doors? We would knock on the door, and hopefully the owner would give us leftovers." She waited, not out of pain but out of reflection. "After a while, it never even occurred to us to wonder who had taken bites out of the food we were eating. When you are hungry, you just do not ask those kinds of questions.

"I slept outside on the ground under verandahs. Life was ..." her voice trailed off. I had been so focused on what she was saying that it was only now when she paused that I noticed again the rain pounding on the roof. "You don't sleep well when you are on the streets. You are kind of half-sleeping and half-listening all the time. You try to rest, and you hope no one is coming."

Out of the corner of my eye I saw the rain pouring down outside. I asked myself what it would be like to sleep even one night outside in this weather. Then I asked myself what it would be like to sleep outside in a place I did not know.

"Life was difficult. It seemed it would go on forever. I had no chance to change my life. All I saw around me was poverty and danger. I thought it was a hopeless existence. It's an awful feeling, being so young and trapped in life with no way to speed up time."

I remembered a similar feeling while living with my grandmother. The days were long. And when you can't sleep, the nights are even longer.

"One day I heard was man coming to our village. News travels fast in slums. Bad news travels very fast. Why, I don't know. Maybe we want to be aware of danger so we can protect ourselves. Good news travels slower. But great news—truly incredible and amazing news—travels the fastest. I think it is this way because it provides hope. And hope for the hopeless is like water in the desert. It reaches what you have been longing for—the possibility that life can be different. That it may in fact be possible to escape the impossible situation you are locked in."

Through all of what she shared, she did not look angry. Instead, she had a peace about her that indicated she had long since forgiven anyone or anything she might have held responsible for her suffering.

"They said he was once a very rich man who sold everything he had to help poor children. The moment I heard it, I believed it. Probably because I wanted to believe it. When you are young and desperate, it is easy to get caught up in something that will provide a way out. But then I got to thinking—why would a rich person do something like this?

"I saw a team of people, all wearing clean T-shirts. They were orange. I love that colour. It spoke of hope and life. Their smiles and their eyes told me they were genuine people coming to help. They gave food to anyone who wanted it. For free. As I came forward I saw a man who was helping to hand out food. And I wanted to find the man responsible for all of this. And someone pointed to the man and said this was Charles Mulli. And I thought, this does not make sense. He is the boss. Why is he here? Why is he giving food? But the moment I saw him, I knew why."

I thought back to when I met Daddy Mulli for the first time. He was unlike anyone I had ever met before. I had the feeling it was a divine appointment. That the date and place of our meeting had been set a long time ago.

"The moment I saw him, I felt I had known him my whole life. He walked up to me and spoke with me. I still can't believe he did that. I was a street child. Alone. I had nothing. And here was this man who could go anywhere in the world and do whatever he wanted. And yet here he was. Talking with me."

She seemed to look through me. It was if she were replaying in her mind the moment she first met Daddy Mulli. I saw in her face the moment of relief that came when she realized Daddy had taken an interest in her. Then her eyes refocused on me, returning to our conversation.

"He asked me to share my story. I told him. Then he asked if I would like to come to live with him." She glanced to the side. A thought had struck her. "You ever think about how many street children there are in Kenya? You can't even count them. And yet he picked me. He chose me. And I tell you, there was nothing that I could give him. Nothing that I could offer to pay him for what he was doing." Her gaze turned back to me. I saw the same peace in her eyes. "He had all the time in the world for me."

She smiled again and then became quiet. The drum of the rain was keeping beat above our heads. We waited, sensing the peace that comes when two people are comfortable with silence.

"I came to MCF Eldoret first and then came here to Ndalani. We are taught many things. To work hard. To study hard. To do our chores. To do karate." She laughed and gave a playful punch in the air. "But you know, the number-one thing we learn is love. To be loved and to love others."

The dorm captain called out, saying it was time for lights out. I was grateful for that. I sensed that Isabella was finished. And that meant my turn to share was coming up. Or not.

"Thank you for sharing," I said.

"Thank you for listening, Hannah," she said. "You are a true friend."

Isabella prayed for us, then pulled herself up to her top bunk. The lights clicked off. I laid my head down on the pillow, listening to the rain, which had somewhat subsided.

As I drifted off to sleep, I thought about all the many difficulties Isabella had faced. I thought about how there wasn't the slightest bitterness or regret in her. And I thought about the joy she had. Her joy was about more than being rescued. Rescue brings relief, but in and of itself it does not bring the kind of glow that she had in her smile. Her tone of voice. Her words.

Her eyes.

Something profound had changed her life. You don't talk about these things the way she had with such optimism, such grace, such hope, without there being a reason for it. She had a joy emanating from her that was full of every good thing imaginable.

And I wanted to find out why.

CHAPTER
fourteen

Considering the hundreds of brothers and sisters I lived with, it was surprising the amount of time I could have to myself. Even with school, choirs, chores, and programs I was involved in, I never felt rushed or hurried. Whenever I needed to think, to reflect, or to be alone with my thoughts, my schedule always made it possible for me to spend time in the quiet. I learned the most when I was in a quiet place, like Thika River.

I heard the birds in the trees talking back and forth with each other in perfect contentment. I felt the wind rustling past me. I saw the simple, elegant beauty of trees around me. And I loved watching the water as it flowed by me. Why is it that I can stare at water so long? What goes by one moment is replaced with a similar yet different pattern a moment later. On and on it goes as it follows the course set out by the riverbanks.

I sat down on the bank, thinking about my conversation with Isabella the night before. She had been through so much, so many difficult trials, and yet she was so content. I thought it might have been because of her personality. Perhaps it was because she was a naturally optimistic person. Perhaps she had told the story so often that she had come to terms with her past.

But the longer I listened to her, the more I saw a vitality in her, a true contentment I did not have. What was it about her that made her that way? Had she realized that her past was really gone and that she had a new life ahead of her? Was it that she had been here longer and that it was only a matter of time for the same thing to happen to me as well?

• • •

After lunch, Isabella and I sat down at our desk. We opened the math textbook we shared and pulled out our notebooks. I gripped my pen and wrote the date in the top right corner. We called the pen a *byro,* and each student carried it carefully because we only had so many to go around. The teachers were very smart. They knew about how long it would take for a pen to run out, so if you went to the supply room and asked for another pen too soon, they would ask what happened to the last one. In this way, we helped to manage our costs, and it set an understanding to take care of what was given to us.

Our teacher entered the room. Unless you were looking in the direction of the door, you would not know she had entered. She had a quiet way about her and a genuine gentle spirit. Her kindness eased my mind and helped me believe that she and I were on the same team, climbing the mountain of the subject together.

She caught my glance. I smiled. She smiled back. It occurred to me that all the pastors, teachers, and other leaders at MCF showed the same love as Daddy Mulli did. Somehow Daddy was able to pick so many people with such a similar outlook on life to serve at MCF.

"Hello, everyone," she said.

"Hello, Miss Washira," we replied.

"Tell me," she said with a quizzical look. "How was your lunch?"

We all said it was very good. And we meant it. When you have lived with so little, it is easy to be thankful for having everything.

"That is good," she said. "That way you have lots of energy for studying."

We laughed. She referred to a problem in our math book and began writing on the chalkboard.

• • •

That evening, I sat in the same desk looking at the same math textbook. I did my best to believe there were other people who also struggled with math, but when it was late and I was still in the class, sometimes I wondered if maybe it was just me.

I exhaled as a sign of frustration. I put my elbows on the table and held up my head with my fingertips. I closed my eyes a moment, rubbing them with the palms of my hands. Maybe a brief break would help.

But if the last number of breaks were any indication, when I reopened my eyes I wasn't suddenly going to get a flash of revelation.

You will never get it.

I can. It just takes time.

Not this long. Anyone else in the world would have gotten it by now.

I heard a slight shuffling of feet at the door. Even though there were dozens of students in my class—47 was the latest count—and even with all those sets of feet coming in and out of the door, I knew exactly who was standing there. When I opened my eyes, I saw her gentle, compassionate expression.

"You are studying late," Miss Washira said.

"I am a little confused," I said. That was only partially true. On a scale between understanding and very confused, I was past the very confused point.

"No problem," she said, sitting down beside me where Isabella usually sat. She talked me through the subject of area. Area is important, she said, if you wanted to know how much farmland you had so you could determine the amount of seed you needed to buy. Area for a rectangle is calculated by multiplying the length times the width. A square is a rectangle with equal sides, but its area is still the length times the width. The area for a circle is pi times the radius squared. Which is the same as saying pi times the radius times the radius again. And don't get confused—there is a difference between a square, which is a shape, and a number squared, which is the number multiplied by itself.

So you can find out the area for the circle. And you can find out the area for a square.

But if you have a circle inside of a square, how do you find the partial area inside the square that is not part of the circle?

I put down my pen.

Starting a journey is a challenge. In the beginning, you have such enthusiasm that you forget how hard it might be. Then, once you have started, all the obstacles show up, and the hint of quitting hangs like a thunderstorm cloud above you.

"This is impossible," I said.

If I was having this much trouble in one class, how much more would I have in all the others, and in all the years to come? The walls felt like they were closing in on me.

"It all depends on how you look at it," Miss Washira said. She smiled. "*Maji hufuata mkondo*," she said in Swahili, which means "water follows its course."

I had heard that common expression before. People said it all the time. But like so many things in life that become routine, I had never really thought about what it meant.

And I wondered how it would apply to me now.

"I do not understand what that expression means," I said.

"When water flows down a river, it follows a natural course. It does not decide to suddenly stop and go uphill. It does not jump up in the air and disobey gravity and chart a course into the sky. Water rushes down a river in a logical, clear path." She spoke in a way that made me know she cared not just about my ability to understand math but about me as a person. I often thought our teachers at MCF were part teacher and part counsellor. "'Water follows its course' means to do things normally—to use your common sense."

"That is all fine and good," I said. "But what if my common sense is not coming to the rescue?"

We laughed so hard, it echoed in the room. It felt good to get a change in emotion. She waited until I turned to meet her gaze.

"Don't worry about formulas. Just look at it and see what you already know. What do you see?"

"I see a circle inside of a square," I said without looking at the picture in the book. I had been looking at it so long I had it etched in my mind.

"Right. And do you know the area of the circle?"

"Pi times the radius squared."

"And do you know the area of the square?"

"Length times width."

Then she did a curious thing. She waited. There are two kinds of waiting. There is the waiting where someone is watching you, judging you, ready to accuse you as soon as you fail. Then there is the other kind of waiting. The waiting where without them saying anything, you feel the encouragement radiating from them into you with the confidence that patience brings.

I looked back at the page. I studied. I concentrated. I let go of all those thoughts of failure.

Nothing seemed to change.

"I don't get it. I am not smart enough."

She paused. "Most things in education are not the result of being smart. They are the result of not giving up. I want to give you a little hint. You don't need to become any smarter. You are already smart. You just need to continue to stay with it. To be willing to be confused for a while. Your mind is processing, and all good things take time."

I looked back at that square with the circle in it.

You will never get it. Just give up.

Just wait. Keep looking. Keep thinking.

It will not make any difference. If it does not come to you easily, it is not worth pursuing.

You are smart. You can get it. Just stay with it.

I kept looking. Kept trying to understand. And then, I saw it. Like a mystery unravelling before my eyes, the solution became clear. Like the sun that rises over Mully Mountain, illuminating the entire MCF grounds, I felt a light shining on this problem. A connection formed in my mind. A bridge from confusion to understanding.

"I subtract the area of the circle from the area of the rectangle," I finally said, breaking what felt like ten minutes of silence.

"Congratulations! You see? You did it."

I calculated the area of the square by multiplying the length times the width. Then I subtracted the area of the circle and reached the answer. I looked over at her. She raised her eyebrows up and then down so quickly that unless you understood the Kenyan way of saying yes you might have missed it. Now that the problem was solved, I wondered why I had worried about it in the first place. Or why I had doubted.

"Thank you."

"You are most welcome. And now it is time for bed."

We walked to the door together. She turned off the light, and we said goodnight to each other. She walked to the teachers' dormitory. I walked to mine. As I saw her leave, I thought to myself how much impact a person can have on someone else.

I walked through the schoolyard and crossed over the bridge; it squeaked as I made it to the other side. I thought about how sharing my math problem with Miss Washira was the starting point to her being able to help me. I needed to open up to her and admit I was struggling. I needed to have the courage to accept her willingness to listen to my problem. And this was good for me to learn.

Because it served as a reminder about what I needed to do next.

• • •

I came into the dormitory later than usual. Even though the light was still on, some of the girls had already gone to sleep. I got ready for bed, and as I was about to enter my bunk, I glanced up to see Isabella in her bed, asleep. That was both good and bad.

See? She's asleep. Don't bother her. Just go to bed.

It's okay. This is important. Tap her on the shoulder. Tell her you need to talk.

Forget this. There is no problem. Everything will work out on its own.

Did your math problem work out on its own? This won't either.

She's exhausted. There will be time tomorrow.

She cares about you. You would do the same for her, wouldn't you?

I got into bed and pulled the cover up to my chin. I laid my head down on my pillow. I looked through the window at the mountain in the distance and waited for the lights to be turned off.

"Hey," a familiar voice from the bunk above me said.

Sometimes that's all it takes for you to snap out of your thoughts. Sometimes one word from a friend can make you realize it might just be time to face those fears.

Just say good night and go to sleep.

She is here for you. She is a good listener.

She won't understand. She's not like you.

Of course she is. You heard her story from last night.

"Hi," I replied.

She came down to my bed and took her familiar place on one end while I sat up on the other.

"You've been busy," Isabella said. "I wanted to see how you are doing."

"Good," I replied.

This is not the right time. Just let it go.

This is the perfect time. You are scared, but you do not need to be.

Just tell her good night and forget all this—

"Thank you for sharing your story with me," I said. "I really appreciated you telling me about your life."

She raised her eyebrows in the way the teacher did a short while before. Then she waited. Patiently. There was no sense of hurry with her. And in this simple gesture—that refusal to wreck a moment with unnecessary words—I felt the total comfort that comes when someone affords you the opportunity to open your heart to them.

I felt the sting of tears beginning to form in the back of my eyes. Instead of trying to hold them back, I let myself feel whatever my heart needed to express. What did I really know about what was going on inside of me, anyway? Are we really the best ones to understand ourselves? Streams of tears rolled down my cheeks and dropped onto the blanket below. If someone asked me to explain why I was crying, I would not have been able to answer. I am sure Isabella knew this. I am sure she knew that people need to heal.

Even if, at the time, they are not aware that they are healing.

Something inside me needed Isabella's listening presence. Something deep in my soul understood that she was safe and that she could be trusted.

Stop! You don't know her!

It is all right. Give her a chance.

To what? To ignore you?

You have been given every reason to know she loves you.

Stop now. Don't tell anyone anything.

Do not be afraid.

I blinked and squished out a rush of tears. It was time to let go of my need to protect my pain.

"I have had a difficult life," I whispered. Those words set off another powerful round of tears that burned around my eyes. I felt the warmth of the stream coming down my face.

Water follows its course.

I looked into Isabella's eyes. I felt invisible strands forming between us, like an ever stronger and growing cord connecting us.

I started from the beginning and told her about everything that had shaped my life. My mother dying. My father dying. My twin sister dying. All the many challenges. All the many questions. All the many details.

I would look directly at her from time to time. My gaze shifted from her to the bedpost, or, more accurately, whenever I was not looking at her I was transferred back to the moment in time, reliving the experiences I was describing to her. I did not know what to expect after I was finished. I had never told anyone my life story before. But each time I chose to continue on, each time I connected by looking into her, I saw someone whose love for me enabled me to release what had been holding me captive.

I admired her. Treasured her. I had felt apprehensive when I started, thinking she might cut me off and deliver well-meaning yet ill-timed advice on how to fix my problems. Instead, she gave me what I needed most. A compassionate, listening ear. And a heart full of love.

What more could I ask for?

She stayed focused on me. She had the ability to make me feel like time had stopped and that nothing—nothing—would deter her from giving me her full and undivided attention.

A person can't fake being genuine.

It brought me relief to know that I did not have to keep everything locked up inside. I could confide in her. I could trust her. I could finally release the pain that was poisoning me all those years.

When I was finished, I felt a strange combination of relief over having finally shared what was on my heart and also curiosity, if not fear, over how Isabella would respond.

There was silence between us. Neither of us felt the pressure to respond. We felt the comfort that comes when people can connect at the deepest level. Daddy said there was power in sharing. He was right. What I did not understand then but came to understand in sharing with Isabella was that he also meant there was power in the person receiving.

And knowing that my heart was understood and received by Isabella gave me such a sense of comfort that it made me wonder why I had waited so long to do this.

"Thank you for trusting me with your story, Hannah," she said. "You have passed through many hard times. And I want you to know that I love you, Hannah. I really love you."

"I love you, too," I said, wiping the last of my tears from my eyes.

That's enough. Fine. You did it. Now go to bed.

I was no longer afraid to be open with her. I had taken the risk. I had shared my whole heart, and she accepted me. So I could ask the question I had been wondering about since I met her.

"Can I ask you something?" I asked.

She raised her eyebrows again.

"You have this peace about you," I said. "Real peace. Can you tell me, where does it come from?"

CHAPTER
fifteen

I focused on Isabella with such intensity that everything else faded out. The security dogs barking outside seemed distant and quiet. The conversations of the girls around us in the other bunks were reduced to a barely audible hum. Isabella and I might as well have been in a desert with nothing around us except sand as far as we could see in any direction.

Sometimes life comes down to moments. This was one of them.

The look on her face was one I had not seen before. There was something deeper, something pressing inside those crystal-clear shells of brown. Her expression made me feel as if she had been waiting for this moment since I first met her. Like everything leading up to this was the climb up a mountain and this was the mountaintop. She had been careful all along not to push her way into my life. Not to force a sunrise before its appointed time. The same gentle calm surrounded her now as it always did. Yet this time the conviction, the life, in her eyes revealed something new. Something more important. I sensed it deep inside of her. Emanating from her heart. Like a glow, a warmth, a peace I had never known.

The peace I wanted.

Not everyone can tell when their heart is in turmoil. Some people become quite skilled at deceiving themselves. They try to avoid coming face to face with their own inability to fill the emptiness of their souls. I had tried to avoid it. But I knew I was empty. There was something both freeing and difficult about coming to this conclusion. I was free because I was honest about my need for peace. And it was difficult because I had to come to the realization I could not fix myself.

My fears and pain had put me into a prison in a bottomless pit. A place I presumed I would stay the rest of my life. Then I met a man named Daddy Mulli. And a woman named Mommy Esther. And a girl named Isabella. And for the first time it occurred to me that I could be set free from my past. From my pain. From my prison. From the person I thought I was destined to remain.

And I felt the hope that comes with realizing life can be different.

"Like you, I have had to go through many challenges," Isabella said. "Our challenges have been different, but both of us were in deep despair after passing through them."

She was right. Our pain connected us. The only difference was that she had somehow let go of her burden of pain, whereas for me it was my daily invisible backpack that seemed to get heavier no matter how much I tried to ignore it.

Isabella tilted her head slightly in her shy, genuine way. "I asked myself, why did all these things happen to me? Why did I have to go through this? I could not understand why."

Neither could I. Life felt like the pieces of a puzzle that drop down to the floor, and as you try to put the pieces together you realize you don't have the picture and you can't make sense of any of it.

"Then I saw Daddy Mulli," she said. "Every child at MCF can tell you exactly where they were when they met him for the first time. For me, I can still see the street where I was standing when I saw him come up to me. He said he wanted to help me leave the street. My life had been consumed with trying to survive. It never occurred to me that I could be rescued from it. There was something about him, something in him that made him such a kind person. So loving, so full of joy, so full of peace. I later thought, how did he get this way? How does someone forgive the people who have hurt him, and have such love?"

I edged myself closer to Isabella. I turned my head slightly as if to make sure I would hear every word.

"He later told me about why he loves us. About why he has such joy in his life."

Isabella paused. I felt a direct connection with her. Like she could communicate to me without saying anything.

"He told me that God loves me. That God created me. That God thinks about me all the time, and that His thoughts about me are good thoughts. When he told me that, I did not feel alone anymore."

Part of me felt I could reach out and touch God. Like He was more real to me in that instant than Isabella sitting right across from me. I felt Him. Sensed Him. Knew He was around me. Yet at the same time, He felt farther away than ever. Like I was in a crowd of people and briefly caught a glimpse of Him, only to have the hustle and bustle of thousands of people push me in another direction, never to see or feel Him again.

"He told me about Jesus."

And then suddenly that massive crowd vanished. Their disappearance was so quick that it left me wondering if they had even been there at all. The room felt clear again.

"He told me that Jesus loves me." She blinked away tears. She spoke in a whisper. "I wonder if deep down inside, all any orphan wants to hear is that they are loved. When we lose our parents, we lose the closest thing to love we have ever experienced. And when they are gone, we figure that's it. We're on our own now. No love left. Not real love, anyway. At least not for us." She smiled as a tear dropped down her cheek. She wiped it away. "Then along comes Daddy Mulli, telling me that Jesus loves me. And everything changes."

Something had changed in her. She had been where I was, and now she had hope. She was different than me. We had the same past. But a different present.

"How did everything change?" I asked.

"I gave my life to Jesus. He changed it for me."

"How did you give your life to Jesus?" I asked.

"He died on a cross for all my sins. I asked Him to forgive me, and I believed in Him to make me a child of God."

I did not understand that. Why would someone have to die for me? When you have been around dying as much as I had been, dying is really the last thing you want someone to have to do for you.

She read my confused expression. Sometimes she could tell what I was thinking even before I could.

"You have a lot of questions," she said with a smile. Then she became quiet. "There is lots of time for questions. Sometimes things happen that we understand, and sometimes things happen that we don't understand. But the most important thing is that you know how much Jesus loves you. Just the way you are. Right here. Right now. There is nothing you need to do to impress Him. Nothing you need to do to get Him to love you. He loves you with all His heart." I felt my eyes begin to sting with tears. "How does that sound?" she asked.

"It sounds pretty good," I whispered. "Thank you, Isabella."

"*Lala salama,*" she said, meaning "good night."

"Lala salama."

She smiled again. And just before she climbed up to her bunk bed, she saw the mist of a tear forming on my eyes. She gave me a hug. "I am so glad you are here," she said. I nodded as she let go. I would have said something if I could. But sometimes when you are shy you don't know what to say.

The lights turned out. I got under my covers and felt the comfort that comes with being in bed.

But I kept thinking about what Isabella had told me. *Jesus loves you.* And the more I thought about it, the more real it seemed.

It became quiet in the room. Everyone had settled in for the night. Everyone except me. That thought stayed with me. *A child of God.*

Jesus, I prayed, *Thank You that You love me. Isabella said that I can become a child of God. How does that happen exactly?*

The village of Umer, where Hannah grew up

The road leading to Mully Children's Family Ndalani

Charles Mulli standing at Jacob's Well, where God provided fresh water for the children at Mully Children's Family Ndalani

The chapel area at Mully Childrens Family Ndalani, where Hannah met Daddy Mulli for the first time

A typical girls' dorm at Mully Children's Family Ndalani, where Hannah and Isabella had many conversations

Students in school at Mully Children's Family Ndalani

Pride Rock

An umbrella thorn tree at Mully Children's Family

The Children's Centre at Mully Children's Family Yatta

Kibera slum

CHAPTER
sixteen

I poured a bucket of water onto the base of a newly planted umbrella thorn tree near the Thika River. The early morning sun glistened off the water as it seeped into the ground, disappearing into the roots below. I admired this type of tree so much. It was easily my favourite. When people think of Africa, this is the aptly named tree that usually comes to their mind. It has a sparse bottom, but the top is flat and the branches stretch out, giving it the form of an umbrella.

There is something so majestic, elegant, and mysterious about the umbrella thorn. Perhaps the tree's ability to shelter people from the sun and rain is what drew me to it. It is so unique that you cannot mistake it for any other tree. Its very existence speaks for itself. Its mysterious and majestic beauty calls out. It does not need anything added to it, and you would not want to take anything away.

It was one of thousands of trees that had been planted on MCF property. The seedlings grew in greenhouses donated to MCF. When they grew large enough, we planted many of the trees on our property; many others we gave away to the community. The Machakos area was a semi-arid region, so we did not get much rainfall. At first glance, a person coming to Machakos would think it to be an impossible land, a lost cause. It seemed far too dry for growing trees and crops. And it was an especially poor location to raise so many children. Yet Daddy Mulli followed the call he received and refused the very notion of impossible.

Planting so many trees created a microclimate and transformed the weather. The impossible could become possible. Where some saw Ndalani as a dry and difficult area, Daddy Mulli saw a future home for all of us.

In a similar way, people drove their cars in the city and saw the street children as an impossible situation. But Daddy Mulli saw a future doctor, a future teacher, a future farmer. More than that, he saw someone who could be transformed. He saw this in me when we first met at the outdoor evening devotional area. Where I doubted, he had faith. Where I saw impossibility, he saw possibility.

His love for me was bigger than my love for myself.

When Daddy Mulli first came to Ndalani, the people there loved him. They had heard of the great Charles Mulli. They thought this wealthy man was coming to bring development to their community.

He was.

But it was a different kind of development than they expected. When people learned that he was going to bring street children to the land, they were ready to throw him out. But he convinced them not to. And he became their most treasured inhabitant.

I stood back and looked at the tree. I could have stood there for hours. Every person has at least something in nature that captures their attention. And for me the umbrella thorn was one of them. I felt inspired as I gazed at it. Captured by it. Humbled by its elegance. Even though it was one among many, it was still unique. It would produce its own leaves to provide beauty for years to come.

Down below I saw the clearing where Mommy Esther taught us about being women of God. *You can see the trees around you. They draw their strength from the water through their roots. In the same way, we trust God to give us His strength into our lives to accomplish His purpose.*

I walked up towards the food preparation table at the back of the devotional area. I heard the incomparable sound of children laughing. I thought I recognized one of the giggles. I smiled as I turned the corner. Sure enough, Zemira, and two younger girls—I guessed they were five years old—had finished their classes and joked with each other as they walked up to their dormitory.

"Hello," I said.

Zemira smiled and gave me a big hug. I turned to the two younger girls.

"How was your day today?"

"Very fine," the taller one said with a big smile and bright brown eyes. The shorter one remained quiet. I could tell she was shy; she reminded me of myself.

I invited them to sit down with me near the tap where we wash our dishes after meals. They giggled as they patted their feet on the ground. I loved the feeling of being with them. The world always seemed right when I had children around me.

"I am wondering if you like to sing songs."

That brought a smile to the shy girl's face. They both nodded.

"Should we sing a song?" I asked.

They nodded again. This time with even more enthusiasm.

"All right," I continued. "But first I need to know your names. Because I think I already know this girl here," I said, playfully pushing Zemira.

"How do you know her?" the louder one said.

"Because she is my sister. Just like both of you. The only thing is that I know Zemira's name but I don't know your names. So what do you think? Do you think we sisters should know each other's names?"

"I'm Doris," the louder one said, laughing. "And this is Susan."

"Doris and Susan. Those are wonderful names. Zemira and I are so glad to spend time with you. Would you like to know my name?" They nodded. "My name is Hannah. Can you say that?"

"Hannah," they replied.

"Very good. I am proud of you. I would like to know, would you like to sing a song where we can clap?"

"Yes!"

"Very good. I think I know just the one."

Amenitendeya *He has done it for me.*
Emmanuel amenitendea *Emmanuel, He has done it for me.*

"That is excellent singing! You both sing very well."

"Thank you," Susan said.

I hugged them both. "And remember, singing reminds us that God is always here to help us. So you sing as often as you like. How does that sound?"

"That sounds very good," Doris shouted. Susan giggled.

Zemira and I glanced at each other.

"It's time for swimming," Doris said. "Come on!"

We cheered as we ran off to our dormitories. As they went to theirs and I to mine, I wondered if they would remember that simple singing together moment. I hoped I would. Even if my mind forgot, I sensed my heart would not. To me it seems that buried within us is an unseen record of the love we have been shown. We are shaped by each of those moments. Spending time with Zemira and these two children reminded me that in each and every moment I wanted to be able to show someone that they were cared for, loved, and appreciated. Like the way Daddy Mulli showed love to me.

• • •

When I turned 14, I became a dorm captain at MCF. There are boys' dormitories and girls' dormitories at MCF. The dorm where I served as captain had about 30 children aged 5 to 12 years old. We had about 10 bunk beds. Sometimes we had more children than beds, and so we slept two on the top bunk and two on the bottom bunk. When there were two to a mattress, we slept head to foot. It got crowded, but no one ever complained. We all knew where we came from.

There are two dorm captains per dorm. The older dorm captain sleeps in a separate room, and I, as the junior dorm captain, slept in the same area as the kids. All the beds had a mosquito net. During the daytime, it is folded up or gets washed.

Each night, before we went to bed, we sang worship songs and prayed together. We would sit on the floor in a circle. Seeing all the girls together is the most precious sight. I got to have Doris and Susan in my dorm. They would sit down on either side of me. I would put one arm around each of them and give them each a hug. That, of course, set off a chain reaction, and each child wanted a hug. They stretched out their arms and walked up to me. Sometimes we even had group hugs where we all just hug each other. Everyone feels better after a hug. Children are no exception. I hugged them and then sat down.

"I would like to know, who has had a good day today?"

They all raised their hands.

"Who learned some good things in school today?"

They kept their hands up and raised them even higher.

"And I would like to know … We are here in this room. You can look around, and you can see what we have. Who here has a nice bed to sleep in?"

"Me!" they shouted.

"Yes, we all have a wonderful bed to sleep in. Who gave us these beds? And who gave us the classrooms, and who gave us this wonderful place to live?"

"Daddy Mulli."

"That's right. And who works through Daddy Mulli to do all this work?"

"Jesus."

"That's right. Jesus is the one who lets us live here. Jesus loves you, and Jesus loves me. And He has a good plan for each of us. How does that sound?"

"Good."

"Very good. Should we sing a song together?"

They clapped and nodded their heads. Some of them were getting tired. I saw them yawn.

"All right. We will sing the song 'Pambio' together; is that good?" They nodded.

Ametenda maajabu nasiwezi kueleza	*He has done so much for me, and I cannot tell it all.*
Ameniokoa mimi nasiwezi kueleza	*He has saved me, and I cannot tell it all.*
Amenipa uhai nasiwezi kueleza	*He has given me life, and I cannot tell it all.*

It warmed my heart to hear the little children singing. They were full of such joy and honesty. Their lives had not been easy, either. Yet there was something precious about young children trusting God in spite of what happened. The troubles of their lives are often a mystery. And I, for one, was not going to try to solve those mysteries with skills I did not possess. I didn't know everything Jesus meant when He said that we had to change and become like little children to enter the kingdom of heaven. But part of it was letting go of our need to have everything explained to us, and to trust and worship God.

"Very good singing," I said with a few quiet claps of my hand. A few of the children clapped as well. "You can all sing so well already. And now let's fold our hands and pray." All the children did as I had asked. They bowed their little heads and clasped their little hands together. Some of them lifted their heads for a moment and looked around, just to make sure they were doing it the right way.

"Thank You, God, for a wonderful day. Thank You for looking after us. Please help us to have a good sleep."

We said good night to each other. I watched the children get into their beds. I tucked the smallest ones in. When they had all found their place, I turned off the light and lay down in my bunk. I pulled the cover up and closed my eyes, assuming it would be quiet, uneventful night.

But it would not turn out that way.

• • •

Sometime during the night, one of the girls called out. At first I wasn't sure if I was dreaming. I was in that strange place between wakefulness and sleep where things become blurred. When she shouted again, I sat up instantly.

I got out of bed and turned on the light, wondering who was having the nightmare. I knew their voices. But when someone shouts, it is harder to determine who is in trouble. I looked around the bunk beds through the mosquito netting, trying to find out who it was. Everyone had woken and were sitting up in their beds.

It was the sound of crying that led me to Susan, shy Susan.

I opened the mosquito netting and sat down on Susan's bed. Her forehead was damp with sweat, her eyes filled with worry. I pulled her onto my lap and felt her shoulders tremble as I hugged her. The dream world can be so powerful that even the presence of light and another person isn't enough to immediately dispel the anxiety of what seemed so real just a moment ago.

"Everything will be all right, Susan," I whispered.

In that moment, I struggled internally with my own beliefs.

Everything will not be all right. Why would you assume that? Why would you lie to a child?

I am not lying. I am speaking the truth. The child's bad dream will disappear.

It will not. It will come right back the moment you put her back to bed.

"What happened, Susan?"

She breathed in short, erratic bursts. I rocked her gently, assuring her that wherever she had been was now far enough away that it could not hurt her.

"I am scared," she said.

"I understand. But we are all here together, and there is nothing to be afraid of."

Sure there is. There are your empty promises, for starters. You guarantee this child security because you think that's what you are supposed to say. But it does nothing for her.

I do not need to worry about my promises. I have God's promises. I do not need more.

"Susan, can I pray with you?" Susan nodded. "Dear God, You see the thoughts that have been in Susan's dream. We know that You are more powerful that anything. And so we pray that You will speak peace to Susan, to clear her mind, and to help her to fall asleep with only Your good dreams. Amen."

I felt her breathing return to a normal pace. I touched her forehead. It was dry.

"Is that better?" I asked.

"Thank you, Hannah," she said as she nodded.

"You are welcome."

I helped her lie back down. I closed the mosquito netting and glanced around to see that the other children had also gone to back to sleep. I was about to leave when I heard her soft voice.

"Hannah?" she said in a faint whisper.

"Yes, Susan."

She pressed her lips together, trying to draw courage.

"What can I do for you, Susan?" I asked.

"Can you stay here?"

"Of course. But can you close your eyes?" I said with a smile. "Is that a deal?"

She nodded.

"I will turn off the light and come right back, all right?"

She nodded again. I went to the door and clicked off the light and came back to her bedside. She closed her eyes and fell asleep. I waited until I heard her breathing pattern change to that deeper sleep sound. I went back to my bed.

You think you helped her? You didn't help at all.

God helped.

You don't know that.

Of course I do. I prayed for God to help her.

And how do you know that your prayer made any difference?

Because that is what prayer does. It makes a difference. Why would I pray and not believe that what I am praying for will happen? I believe God will answer my prayers.

I laid my head down on the pillow. As I drifted off to sleep, I thought that we would now have a peaceful night.

That would be true for the rest of the girls in the room.

But it would not be that way for me.

• • •

I stood up and felt the cold concrete floor under my bare feet. The air felt cold too. That wasn't unusual, though. Even in Kenya, the nights can become chilly. I rubbed my shoulders to warm myself. The dark of night was so deep that I had to squint to see the end of the room. I expected to see the wall there. I *should* have seen the wall there. But instead I saw a forest. Long trunks of trees filled the landscape with branches becoming thicker the higher they went. I walked to the end of room, peering deeper and deeper into the forest. When I reached the edge of the room and looked around, the forest stretched out as far as I could see. My toes touched soil, but the soles of my feet stayed resting on concrete.

I saw my breath in the cold night air. Part of me knew I could walk back to the dormitory. But the other part of me knew I was supposed to walk forward.

I swallowed.

I took a step.

My eyes opened. I felt my heart beating. I sat up in bed and grabbed the wooden frame as a feeble attempt to assure myself I was no longer in the forest.

Or was I?

You see? Your prayers might work for a little girl. But there is no help for you.

I grabbed my blanket and wrapped it around myself.

Please God. Please help me.

There is no help for you. God will not help you. If He did help, He would not have given you this dream.

Our God is our refuge and strength. An ever present help in the time of trouble.

Your troubles are only beginning. There is no one here to pray for you. Only little children. Little girls. What are you going to do now? Are you going to wake them up? Is that what you will do? Plead and beg with them to pray for you be rid of your nightmares?

Please God. You are all that I have. It is late, and I don't know who else to turn to. I am so afraid. I don't want a dream like this. Please remove it from me. Help me to sleep well. You are the only one who can help me.

Suddenly, the other voice was gone. In that instant, the room felt altogether different. Like it had been years since I was in that forest. It seemed like a distant memory. The room felt comfortable again. My heart was still and quiet within me.

Thank You, God. Thank You.

It was one thing to pray for Susan and to see her sleep well. It was something different when I had to pray for myself. And yet, the result was the same. As I lay back down, I drifted off to sleep. If I had other dreams after that, I can't recall what they were. I slept all the way until daybreak.

• • •

The clanging sound of the handbell at six o'clock told me it was time to wake up. My first reaction that morning, and every morning, was to pray in my bed. *Thank You, Lord, for this new day. Help me in all my duties today. Help me to listen to You. Help me to encourage the children.*

The dorm captain and I got our 30 children ready for school. We combed their hair, got them dressed, prayed with them, encouraged them. You've never seen anything so funny in all your life as our morning routine. We had done it hundreds of times, yet as any mother will tell you, when children are involved, it is always an adventure. Yes, it was a busy time, but it was also a great time, the way things always are whenever I forget about myself and focus on serving others.

The children put on their sandals. We counted their heads, and, reaching 30, we led them off to breakfast.

"So Doris," I said on our way. "I wonder who is the faster runner—you or Susan?"

"That is a good question," Doris asked. "But it is not the most important question."

"Really?" I asked. "And what is the most important question?"

"The real question is—who is faster, Doris, Susan ... or you?"

And with that the two children raced out ahead of me. The other children hurried after them. I ran with them, hearing their giggles as their little feet carried them along the ground.

"Wow! You guys are doing great!"

I ran alongside them. Doris and Susan reached the children's centre first.

"Perfect!" I said. "Now we are all good and hungry for breakfast!"

The children queued up in the line. We sat down at tables in the children's centre and ate our breakfast together. I watched to make sure everyone was eating and that everyone had enough.

After breakfast, we helped the children get ready for school. As they left the dormitory for their classes, I heard a familiar voice behind me.

"Hello, Hannah."

Voices are more than just sound. They carry with them the entire essence of the person speaking. You ever notice that no two people say your name exactly the same way? They can't. Because no two people are alike. I loved hearing my name. Especially from Daddy Mulli. Simply hearing his voice put me at total peace.

I turned around. His bright smile outshone the Kenyan sun.

"Hello, Daddy."

"I am so glad to see you again, Hannah. Did you get enough to eat?"

As an abandoned child, Daddy knew all about what it meant not to have enough to eat. Whenever there was a drought, Daddy Mulli would invite the entire community to come to MCF for a feeding program. So when he saw us after breakfast or when he saw community people coming to eat, Daddy would always ask, Did you get enough to eat?

"Yes, Daddy. Thank you."

"Great. I see that you are very good with the children."

"You think so?"

"Oh, yes. You really love them. And you know, I can tell that they really love you, too."

"Thank you, Daddy."

"And so, I have a question for you. I would like for you to come with me to visit Yatta. What do you think?"

Yatta is an area about a half-hour drive from Ndalani. Daddy Mulli started MCF Yatta to care specifically for girls, who come from every difficult situation imaginable. It is home to hundreds of former orphaned street girls and to single mothers with babies.

In Kenya, we do not have welfare or social assistance. If you are pregnant, and if you have no husband, and if your family abandons you, then you are doomed. There is no money you can collect from the government. There is no place you can go for help. We don't have those privileges here. If you find yourself in that kind of trouble, you will be left to do whatever you can for yourself and your young one. You may have to beg. You may have to steal. And like many, you may have to resort to doing anything to survive. The unbearable shame and the unwillingness of others to help are enough to corrupt whatever clear thinking you might have left. Being a single, poor, pregnant mother causes physical, mental, and emotional stress that can drive you mad.

It is desperation on every front.

It is the definition of a complete disaster.

Unless, of course, you meet a man named Charles Mulli and he invites you to MCF Yatta.

CHAPTER
seventeen

The road from MCF Ndalani to MCF Yatta was bumpy and beautiful. The mountains of Ndalani eventually gave way to the flatter area of Yatta. It surprised me how quickly the landscape changed. Perhaps it served as a reminder to us that if the landscape could change, then perhaps the people living in it could too.

I gazed out the window of the MCF van travelling through the countryside. I could watch for hours. I found nature comforting. I heard God speak to me through His creation. It's been said that a picture is worth a thousand words. In Africa, I think it's more like ten thousand words.

Farmland surrounded us on both sides. I saw the faces of people who ran up to us whenever we stopped. They tried to sell us mangos, bananas, and soft drinks. I admired their determination, and I wished I had money to give to everyone who needed it.

We turned left off the highway to the road leading to MCF Yatta. I saw row after row of massive greenhouses lining the road. Each one was big enough to fit a football field inside. MCF grew a million tree seedlings each year, in addition to other plants. On the other side of the road, the horizon was filled with farm after farm of French beans. MCF grew many other crops, including cucumbers, cabbage, kale, spinach, tomatoes, maize, *capsicum* (peppers), and onions.

Farther down the road, I saw the large administration building, surrounded by a security wall. We waved to the guard, who opened the black gate and let us onto the property. We came to a stop at the front of the building, and I stepped out.

It was difficult to believe what I saw. I did not know what to expect at MCF Yatta. Sometimes we build ideas of what the places we are going to visit will be like. Then after being there, we debate about whether that place met our expectations or not. But after coming to MCF Ndalani, I realized that I would never have been able to imagine something so incredible. And coming to MCF Yatta for the first time, I was just as curious about what God had built there.

If you told people the property used to be barren land only a few years before, they might have a hard time understanding it. I gazed around and saw the incredible development. I saw schools, a centre for little babies, and dormitories. I could hardly believe this place was real. Daddy Mulli once said MCF felt like a dreamland. It was just what I thought when I first arrived. "Impossibility is nothing with God," Daddy Mulli had said. Even though there were many examples to prove his point, this place alone was enough for me to believe this statement.

I wonder if Daddy Mulli envisioned MCF to be this incredible when he first decided to sell everything he had to rescue kids like me. I wonder if when he was at that bridge on the way to Uganda—when he was struggling to make the incredible decision years ago whether to stay in business or give it up to start this ministry—did he already see all of this? Or was it all a step of faith?

As we walked towards the school we met people along the way. Daddy Mulli would stop and greet each person by name. With each step, I saw more buildings, more people working. I sometimes wonder what took more courage—to start a place like this or to run it?

I thought of the story in the Bible of the priests bearing the ark of the Lord. When their feet touched the Jordan River, God parted the waters for the children of Israel to pass through to Jericho. In many ways, Yatta became Jericho for the women who lived here.

As we walked past a large water tower, I looked to my left and saw smoke rising from a large pot in the kitchen. A man stirred the contents with a large ladle, using both arms. The metal walls of the kitchen and the fire burning below made it seem unbearably hot. I saw how hard he worked to make food for hundreds of people, serving faithfully in relative obscurity. Daddy Mulli noticed him too, of course. Daddy said hello and called him by his name. The man smiled and waved back.

To the right, I saw a long row of dormitories. "This is where all the new girls are living," Daddy said. I saw a number of girls standing around their new homes. I was eager to meet them. Daddy walked towards them, giving a friendly wave. As we got closer, I felt something I had not felt in a long time. I swallowed, hoping what I was seeing was not correct. When we reached them, I suddenly understood what I was seeing.

Everyone who has felt hopelessness can recognize it when they see it.

The girls had an undeniable vacant stare in their eyes. If you looked long enough you could see the rank depression, fear, and anger inside of them. I had never seen people so devoid of life. From far away they looked just like anyone else. But up close, their eyes looked like empty shells—like the pain of life had long since taken away whatever joy might have once been there.

One girl had such short hair it was almost not there at all. She hunched over as if in pain. She moved slowly. All of them did.

It seemed to me that they had reached the absolute end of whatever journey they had been on and simply did not have the energy, or the will, to carry on. It was puzzling at first. Why would there not be life in their eyes if they knew they were now here? Was MCF Yatta not an immediate beacon of hope to those who only hours ago were living on the streets at the bottom of the world? If someone were adrift at sea for days in a faltering lifeboat in the sweltering sun, would there not be an immediate relief once they were rescued?

But sometimes good news is not enough to revive a person. And the more I looked, the more I realized that, even in my own life, healing was a process.

I had a hard time imagining what these girls would look like if they were happy. I am guessing some were 16; some might have been younger. It was difficult to tell. A hard life ages a person more quickly. The sheer weight of the deadness in their eyes made it impossible for me to imagine what they might have looked like otherwise.

It took people like Charles Mulli to see what was not there.

To see what could be there.

To see what *would* be there.

I said hello to one of them. Even though she was within hearing distance, she gave no indication she heard. Her pain was so deep that even a simple hello became a burden. Daddy Mulli approached her. He called her Johari, a Swahili name meaning "gem or something of value." He spoke to her with his kind, gentle demeanour, with a tone that had a way of reaching not simply your ears but your soul as well. She looked off at no place in particular, trying her best to recover from whatever world she had just been rescued from.

One of the workers at MCF explained to me that Johari had been living on the streets with her baby. MCF rescued both of them, and her child was now at the mother-daughter centre at Yatta.

I tried to imagine what she was thinking and feeling. There must have been a flux of emotions running through her. As I watched Daddy speaking with her, I saw a brief shift in her expression. It was as if for just a moment someone had turned the light on inside her to bring her back to life, similar to the way the headlights of a car flicker when a dead battery begins to be charged.

• • •

I wanted to help her. I wanted to ease the trauma in her mind. To assure her that no matter how confusing and impossible the world looked, it was possible to have a new life. The compassion, the conviction, and the care with which Daddy Mulli spoke to her so inspired me. I wondered if I could be used in the same way.

Daddy Mulli said goodbye to her as she left with one of the teachers to join her class. Each girl in Yatta has the opportunity to go to high school and to attend a vocational school. They can choose to study hairdressing, beauty therapy, tailoring, dressmaking, home economics, entrepreneurship, evangelism, and computer courses. The mothers go to school during the day while their babies or school-aged children are cared for in the baby centre or in primary school. This gives the women an opportunity to learn the skills they need to earn a living and to be able to care for their children.

We turned down to the left, and I looked out at the massive earth dams. MCF built these to support fish, livestock, and farming activities to become self-sustainable. The water from the dams also provided support for producing a million tree seedlings each year to assist in the MCF climate change program.

As we walked down, we came to the children's centre. It was a humble red building with a playground enclosed in a fence. We opened the gate. Children ran and played everywhere, swaying on the swings and sliding down the slide. I saw a baby, maybe nine months old, standing on wobbly legs at the door of the school, being helped by an adult. The baby wore a white shirt and white shorts and had big, shy eyes. I knelt, keeping my distance to give her whatever time she needed to warm up to me, and I smiled at her.

She smiled back, then looked down to the ground.

"Hello. Hello," I said. She looked up into my eyes, then back at the teacher she was with, as if to confirm this was all right. The teacher smiled at her.

"Her name is Akachi," the teacher said. The name means "God's hand."

"Hello, Akachi," I said. I approached her. She held out her arms. I lifted her up. "I am so glad to meet you. My name is Hannah. You are a wonderful young girl."

She scrunched her nose up, wiggling in my arms to get a better look at my eyes. She looked into me, and I into her, and both of us felt the joy that comes from communicating without words.

"What would you like to do? Where should we go?"

She turned around and pointed into the building. I carried Akachi inside. I saw small children's classrooms on either side of a narrow hallway. The rooms were full of little chairs and small tables. Bible verses were written on the walls.

I walked with Akachi to the back of the building. Mattresses lay on the ground, covering the entire floor. Young children slept on them during their afternoon naps.

Daddy left me to spend the afternoon playing with Akachi. I sang to her and told her stories from the Bible. Mostly I just held her, the future generation. I felt as if I were holding a baby of my own.

Three hours later, Daddy Mulli came back.

"I see you have met Akachi," he said with a big smile. If Akachi took to me, she took even more to Daddy Mulli. She stretched out her arms and jumped into him. He took her in his arms and laughed. Akachi laughed too. "Do you know whose child this is?" he asked. I shook my head. "This is Johari's daughter."

• • •

I came back to Yatta often. I played with the children, especially little Akachi. I read to the children and prayed with them. I sometimes wondered who did more for whom. I came to offer any help I could to the children, but I always left having received more than I gave. One day, over lunchtime, I saw Johari approaching the baby centre. I recognized her from a distance. At least I thought I did.

"Hello, Akachi!" she said, picking up her daughter. "How are you?"

I had a hard time believing she was the woman with the vacant stare I had seen the first time I came to Yatta. Her eyes had become so bright. It was as if that car battery was not only charged but replaced with one ten times stronger. *Radiant* is the only way I could describe her. She laughed with a genuine laugh as Akachi patted her face and scrunched her nose.

Johari cuddled her daughter.

"Thank you so much for looking after her," she said.

"You are welcome."

"How are you doing? How is life at MCF Ndalani?"

"It is fine. Thank you. MCF Ndalani is going very well."

Johari sang a brief song to little Akachi. Then she turned to me. "Your studies are going well?" she asked.

"They are going well. And you?"

"Incredible," she said. "The Lord is doing great things." She touched Akachi on the nose. "Isn't that right? Isn't that right, Akachi?"

Akachi laughed.

She asked what I wanted to become, and I shared my dream of becoming a doctor. She told me it was a wonderful goal. I hugged them both. As I walked up the hill, I turned back to see mother and daughter together. The impossible had become possible.

I got back on the bus. We drove down the road to the highway and began the bumpy, beautiful journey back. The large fields of Yatta eventually gave way to the mountains of Ndalani.

Landscapes change.

CHAPTER
eighteen

The rhythm of our feet dancing on the classroom's concrete floor filled the evening air. Our sandals swished in a repeating pattern, sending out the beat for our song. We swayed together from side to side in perfect unison as if we were a forest of trees with the wind passing through us. Our voices blended together, making our group of 24 sound like many more. Singing together felt so natural. Freeing. Energizing.

After a full day of classes, chores, and studying, choir practice gave me the perfect end to my day. This day in particular was special. Because tonight, I would be singing the solo part in a song for the first time.

I closed my eyes. I felt a tingling in my toes, a rush of warmth racing through me. The concerns of the day disappeared. I felt at total peace. A smile came on my face without any effort from me. I felt like I could stay this way forever, making me wonder if maybe this was what heaven might be like.

This is what we sang:

Hakuna Mungu Kama wewe.   *There's no one, there's no one like Jesus.*

Hakuna na hata kuwepo.	*There's no one, there's no one like Him.*
Nemetembea—kote kote!	*I walked and walked all over, over!*
Nimetafuta—kote kote!	*I searched and searched all over, over!*
Nimezunguka—kote kote!	*I looked around all over, over!*
Hakuna na hata kuwepo.	*There's no one, there's no one like Him.*

Even though we sang a large number of songs, for me the hour-long practices felt like they were only minutes long. When Dickson announced choir practice was over, I felt my jaw drop. Already? Why does time pass so quickly when you are doing something you love? It served as another reason why heaven will be so great. Eternity is lots of time do the things we love.

I stayed behind again that evening. By myself. In the choir room. I soaked up the lingering feeling in the air after everyone had left. Interesting how a room can feel a certain way depending on what just happened inside of it. Singing about Christ changed the room. Changed the evening. Changed my heart. I felt Him in the room. What was once four walls, a roof, and a concrete floor had become a hallowed and joyful place of worship.

Standing here made me think there must be many ways to describe worship. How could a person ever find enough words to do justice to what it means to be in God's presence? During the choir practice, I felt the most incredible sense of love and freedom. It made me feel that I was the person I was designed to be.

I walked out of the classroom, wishing instead I could have stayed there longer. I took the steps down to the ground and looked up at the beautiful night sky. Stars flooded the canopy above from end to end. *I am at MCF,* I thought. *I am at the best place in the world.* The longer I gazed up, the more I had the undeniable sense that even as each of the stars had their precise spot where they were meant to shine, I too had my place in the universe. That God had planted me here, in this place, in this time, to shine for Him. It comforted me to know I was not here by chance.

As I crossed the bridge, I saw Daddy Mulli finishing a conversation with one of the pastors. He always worked, yet he never appeared tired. Despite his many challenges, he always had time for people. He said good-night to the pastor. I turned and walked into the shadows en route to my dormitory. It was late. I did not want my father to feel obligated to speak with me after what I am sure was yet another busy day for him.

"Hello, Hannah," he said.

There it was again. The sound of his voice saying my name. I turned. Daddy Mulli walked towards me with his compassionate smile.

"Hi, Daddy," I said.

"I heard you singing all the way over here."

"Really?"

"Oh yes. I did. You sing very well, Hannah. So beautifully."

I smiled, feeling the assurance of his approval. He had a way of knowing exactly what to say and how to say it. It was not just his words. There was more to it. Maybe it was as simple, and as powerful, as the radiance emanating from inside him. I sensed his love for me. A love that accepted me without me needing to do something or become someone other than exactly who I was.

And I think inside every girl's heart is a desire to be approved by her dad.

"Thank you," I whispered.

"I think you really enjoy singing. Tell me, why do you sing? Can you explain what singing does for you?"

I thought a moment. Some people talk out loud to sort out their thoughts. Others like me prefer to organize our thoughts internally so that when we speak they are already formulated. "It is a gift I have, and I love to share it with people." I thought back to the choir practice. I thought about what I felt and *why* I felt it. "When I sing, I feel close to God."

Daddy Mulli nodded in agreement. "God gives us ways in which we can know Him. We see the beautiful stars He created. We sense Him when we sing. We feel His presence in the devotions." His voice trailed off. We stood in the silence. He waited a moment and then continued, "And yet, the only way we can truly come to know God is through His Son, Jesus Christ. Do you understand?"

I did. Wait. Did I? I thought I did. I wasn't sure. I had heard about Jesus every day at MCF. Was that enough?

"There is peace and faith that comes in knowing God. And one of the best ways we come to know Him is by reading the Bible."

Daddy handed me a blue-and-white hardcover book. I thought at first he was showing me a textbook that had interested him. But when I saw how he held the book for me to take, I realized he was giving this book to me. I read the cover.

A Bible.

"This is my gift to you. Reading the Bible is the perfect start or ending to any day. This pattern of reading will help you to think about God's Word during the day as well."

"Thank you," I said.

"God has something good for your life, Hannah. He has a purpose. You saw at Yatta how girls arrive there without any hope. They feel really lost. Completely."

I remembered the vacant look in the eyes of the girls. Johari's in particular. Lifeless. Full of anger. Full of hurt. I couldn't even imagine someone could look like that. Is that how I had looked when I first came to MCF?

"But then they change. They smile. Their eyes become bright. They are transformed. And how? We might ask, how are they transformed? Is it through hard work? Is it because they have a good place to live? Is it because they have a brighter future and will get a job? All of these things are good. But they do not bring true, lasting joy. This is one of the mysteries of life. People chase after things hoping to fill their emptiness, but it does not get better. And yet the girls at Yatta have discovered a secret."

A song came back to me. *Nimegundua siri. Nimegundua siri. Nimegundua siri Ya kukaa ndani ya yesu.* It meant, "I have found a secret. I have found a secret. I have found a secret and it's Jesus in my heart."

"The Bible says, 'the secret of the LORD is for those who fear Him.' So I would like to encourage you to read your Bible."

"All right, Daddy. I will."

"God loves you. And He wants to spend time with you. And do you know why?"

"Why?"

"Because you are precious to Him. How does that sound?"

"Good."

"Very good, then. Another wonderful day here at Mully Children's Family. Wouldn't you say?" he said with a laugh. "I tell you, it was an amazing day. Many days I think, today was a great day. No way that it can ever get better. And then there comes the next day, and it is even better!"

I laughed. "It is very good."

"Yes, very good. The Lord is very good to us. And so, dear Hannah, I wish you a great evening."

"And you too, Daddy."

"Lala salama," he said as we parted ways, meaning "sleep well."

"Lala salama," I replied.

I glanced back at him as he walked away. On the outside, he appeared to be like anyone else. But those of us who knew him, those of us who had the chance to learn about true love from him, would tell you he was unlike anyone we had ever met.

I sometimes wondered if he realized the impact he had on us.

• • •

I sat down on my bed, thinking about what Daddy Mulli had told me. *God loves you. And He wants to spend time with you.* I watched the younger girls as they played in the room before prayer time. Does God love to spend time with me the way I love to spend time with my younger sisters?

I opened my blue-and-white Bible. I flipped through the pages. I found a passage we discussed in Bible study. It is a famous passage. And for good reason. It had become one of my favourites as well. I read Psalm 23 quietly to myself, thinking about what each verse meant.

The LORD is my shepherd, I shall not want.

Shepherds take care of their sheep. This verse told me that God will always be there for me, so I never need to worry. When I lost my parents, I felt alone. Adrift. And yet, since coming to MCF I knew God was with me. Like when Daddy Mulli is around me, everything feels right. And knowing God is around me helps me not to worry. His presence alone gets rid of my fears. His presence is everything I need. My desires for other things disappear when I have God. I do not want or need anything else.

He makes me lie down in green pastures.

God cares about me. He cares about what happens to me. My life matters to Him. He considers me someone worth spending time with. He provides what I need so that I don't have to be anxious about tomorrow.

He leads me beside quiet waters.

God wants what is best for me. This does not mean He wants what is easiest for me. But when I know He is leading me, I know I can rest in Him. His right hand guides me and holds me. God is leading me through everything.

He restores my soul.

Who else can? I sometimes wonder if all of our searching and trying to make life work, and trying to make sense of a world that is too complicated for us, stem from us not relying on God to fix us. Maybe part of the battle is realizing that we are broken to begin with. Sometimes things in life do not work out. But God is my hope when I am hopeless. He is my encouragement. He heals what has been broken.

He guides me in the paths of righteousness for His name's sake.

God leads me in the path that is right for me. His paths are good paths. They are meaningful paths. Sometimes they are paths filled with laughter. Other times they are paths filled with tears and unbearable hurt. But whatever path He puts me on, He makes me more like Him. Who am I to know what kind of a path I should be on? The real question is, am I willing to walk with Him on the path He has called me to? Whatever path it is, I know He will be with me step by step. Do I need to know what will happen down the road? No. No, I do not. I just need to be willing to be humble, honest, and courageous. He is the one who leads, and He alone can make me righteous.

Even though I walk through the valley of the shadow of death, I fear no evil.

God is always with me, even when I pass through difficulties and when I sleep. God's presence drives away fear. Being with God brings me much encouragement. I have nothing to fear with God.

For You are with me; Your rod and Your staff, they comfort me.

Is there a greater promise than God's presence? Jesus says in Matthew, *I am with you always.* I am under His cover. He gives me comfort. And nothing can hurt me where I get comfort.

You prepare a table before me in the presence of my enemies.

I should stop comparing myself with others. It is not right to look at people who might have more than me and determine my worth based on someone else's success. Who created these standards of success anyways? And how do I know that the standard I use is a good one? God alone is the one who sets the only standard. He takes care of me and seeks to build bridges with everyone. Unfortunately, not everyone agrees to sit down at the table He has set. I don't need to compare myself to someone else. I should appreciate myself for who I am. I really am fearfully and wonderfully made. God took the time to design me. To make me into who I am today.

He created us equal before Him. He loves us no matter the tribe we are from, the place we are from, the way we look, the talents we have or don't have, or even the way we behave. A lot of troubles vanish when I realize I am loved no matter what.

You have anointed my head with oil.

I am a blessed person. I am anointed by God.

My cup overflows.

I will never lack, because He is always my provider.

Surely goodness and lovingkindness will follow me all the days of my life.

God has good plans for me that were set before I was born. Plans that will let other people know about who He is and how wonderful He is. My life will be full of blessings, and these blessings will bring other people closer to God.

And I will dwell in the house of the LORD forever.

I had heard this last verse many times. Yet this time it caused me to pause. Sometimes you hear something over and over again, and then one time it suddenly convicts you in a different way.

But what was it? Which part of this verse was speaking to me?

I started at the beginning. Perhaps it was the word *dwell*. To stay with God is the best future imaginable. What could be better? Daddy Mulli gave me a place to dwell. When I compared where I was before and where I was now at MCF, it was truly an amazing difference. Dwelling with all my brothers and sisters was a blessing beyond a blessing. And if living here was so incredible, how much more incredible would it be to dwell with God? But as I read the word *dwell* over and over again, I did not sense any conviction that this was what was troubling me.

Perhaps it was the phrase *in the house of the LORD*. Was that what was impacting me? I understood *in the house of the LORD* to be heaven. What could be better than that? The pastors said there is a heaven and there is a hell. And each of us is going to one of those two places. That sent a shudder through me. The very thought of being apart from God sent my mind to a place I did not want to go.

During the day, all the busyness of life, my siblings, the activities, and the incredible sunshine kept my mind occupied. But later at night, in the quiet of my bed, where there were no distractions, the thought about the house of the Lord became more and more comforting to me. I remembered the joy of being in the devotional area in the evening with the other children. If this was how it felt with my brothers and sisters down here on earth, how much better would it be with them in the house of the Lord?

Forever. Who could really understand forever, anyway? What was forever? Was it time going on and on without end? How could something go on and on? Does it never end? How could something not end? Everything down here on earth has a beginning and an end. I remembered hearing one of the pastors say that *God has set eternity in the human heart.* I sometimes wonder if that meant we each have within us the imprint that we were meant for another place.

I felt a glimpse of forever in choir. When I sang, I felt the absence of time. The effect of time for me only began after choir practice was over. Maybe that's what forever meant: having time, without the consequences of having things end. Perhaps eternity was never meant to be understood down here. Perhaps it was meant to help us know the eternal consequences of whether or not we choose to believe.

So, there was the verse *And I will dwell in the house of the LORD forever.* It was a wonderful verse. It made sense to me. I should have been able to close the Bible and call it a day. Yet I still felt a deep uneasiness about it. I sensed a check in my spirit—something that would not simply allow me to gloss over what was bother me until I came face to face with it. The more I felt it, the more concerned I became. Something about this verse was not resonating with me. It was like being in a choir and I was the only one singing off-key. I had studied this verse. I had thought about it. I had gone through it word by word.

Or had I?

Wait a minute.

There was one word I had not studied. One word my eyes conveniently overlooked. One word I had assumed was not the word that was bothering me. I had assumed it was one of the larger words. But I was wrong. Which word was it?

Not being able to identify it, I read the verse again.

Dwell. In the house of the Lord. Forever. Those all looked fine. But those words were not what gripped my spirit with such unbearable conviction. What was it? What was the problem?

I looked carefully at the beginning. That's when it hit me with such force that I could think of nothing else. I realized what spoke to me, what reached right to the very core of my existence, was the second word in that verse.

I. Me. Hannah. I felt my heart skip a beat. A rush of adrenalin burned through me. I felt as frail and as convicted as I ever had in my entire life.

Am *I* going to dwell in the house of the Lord forever?

Had I missed it? Had I missed everything this verse was telling me? Had I missed the entire purpose of being at MCF? Had I missed the entire reason for the love of Daddy and Mommy Mulli? Had I heard and sung about God and yet missed what it was really all about?

It was as if a curtain had suddenly been opened to let a flood of sunlight into my life. It revealed an emptiness in my heart. Somehow I had always known it was there, but I was unable to define what it was.

Until now.

A deluge of thoughts raced through my mind. Competing voices fought to win me over.

Of course you will dwell in the house of the Lord forever. You are a wonderful person.

What does it really mean for someone to dwell in the house of the Lord forever?

It's been a long day. You are tired. Just put the Bible down and get some rest.

There is a reason why this verse is speaking to me.

Tomorrow is another day. The bright sunshine will make everything feel better. You are making a mountain out of nothing.

The still, small voice you hear is encouraging you. Take care that you pay attention to it. Don't ignore what is being said to you.

If this really were of God, why would you feel this way? God brings peace, does He not? So why do you feel such unrest?

I closed my eyes. I took in a deep breath and exhaled. But it did nothing to assuage the battle going on inside me.

There is nothing you need to do. You have been rescued. You are on the road to becoming a doctor. You have a bright future.

You can't afford to pretend. Not with eternity at stake. In the end, everyone has to respond. This is your opportunity. What does it take for you to dwell in heaven forever? How do you really know for sure that you are going there?

I looked up. It was getting late. I got out of bed. I prayed together with the children and watched as the little precious people got into their beds. I turned out the lights and got back into my bed.

But the thoughts did not leave me.

Will I really dwell in the house of the Lord? Will I get there? Am I just fooling myself about what this is all about?

I felt the tightness in my heart come back. In that moment, I was completely convinced that eternity awaits all of us.

In one place or the other.

I wondered where that would be for me. I thought about Daddy Mulli's words.

The only way we can truly come to know God is through His Son, Jesus Christ. Do you understand?

From the bottom of my heart I sure wished I did. But sitting there in my bed, I had to be honest with myself. No. No, I did not understand. I had thought I did. I had thought I knew exactly. But I was wrong.

Dear God, am I going to heaven? Am I going to be with You?

As I lay down in my bed and put my head on my pillow, I had the unmistakable feeling that I was missing something.

Or, more exactly, that I was missing someone.

CHAPTER
nineteen

S ometimes the familiar can suddenly feel different.

The younger children ran ahead of me to the evening devotional the way they always did. Their energy and excitement brought a smile to my face. They laughed and giggled as they raced each other to reach the front. They hurried to find places on the wooden benches, where their little legs were not able to reach the ground. The stars shone down on me the way they did every clear evening. I saw the leaves of the acacia trees rustle as the wind blew through them. It was a normal evening, like any other. Everything looked the way it usually did.

But it *felt* different.

How could a routine event like this suddenly seem so out of the ordinary? Normally I talked with Isabella, or my other siblings, on the way. But today, even though I walked beside her, we were strangely quiet. Everything became still for me, like everyone else was carrying on with their lives and I was somehow taking hallowed steps. It felt as if I had walked here only a moment ago and had come back to retrace my path.

We sat down under the protection of the overhang. I felt the comfort that came in being together with so many of my siblings while we waited for the singing, praying, and preaching to begin, I loved the feeling of us being together. Children once lost who had now been found.

The few lights above us gave what little illumination we needed to see each other. I glanced around at my siblings. Each person had been given a unique face to match their unique personality, their unique design. We squeezed together on the bench whenever another sibling came looking for a spot. There was always room for another at MCF. Always room for one more in Daddy Mulli's heart.

One of our siblings stood up and walked to the front.

"Praise the Lord," she said.

"Amen," we all responded.

"Praise the Lord again," she said.

"Amen," we replied.

She gave us a word of encouragement and then led us in a rhythm. We stood. Our feet swished against the floor as we moved together as one. We began to sing. Normally I would have felt I was in my element. I would have sung like nothing else in the world mattered. But the words from the day before felt as heavy on my mind now as they had then. *And I will dwell in the house of the Lord forever.*

I had the incredible sense something was not right.

Everything is fine. Just sing your songs, go to evening study, and head to bed like every other evening.

This is not like every other evening. Tonight is different.

Why should it be different? Everything here is going fine. You are doing really well.

Things are not always the way they appear.

Of course they are. Seeing is reality. You know this.

I had sung so many songs, heard so many sermons, and listened to so many testimonies. But there was more going on tonight than on any other evening. We sat down after singing. Everything felt quiet. Unhurried. Still.

• • •

Someone began clapping in rhythm. We all joined in. The timing of our claps matched my heartbeat. The perfect unison was the only sound in an otherwise quiet evening.

One of the pastors stood up. When he reached the stage, we became quiet. Everything went back to a perfect calm. And the moment the pastor said his first word, I felt something I had never felt before.

It was as if he was speaking directly to me.

"God has a good purpose for you."

There are words that reach our ears. Other words reach our mind. Still others reach all the way to our heart. But only a few reach deeper than our heart. These are words that reach our spirit. And this is what I felt when I heard the pastor speaking.

There was no effort in his speech. No sense of him trying to convince me that what he was saying was important. It *was* important. All on its own. He was like a gate being lifted to allow an incredible flow of calm water rush into me. His words were effortless. Easy. Deep. It reminded me of when Daddy Mulli spoke.

"Whatever you have passed through, God has a good plan. We think to ourselves, if God has a good plan, why did things not turn out the way I wanted them to turn out? We can think, if God is a good God, why doesn't everything seem good all the time? Why does He allow difficulties?"

Because God does not care, that's why. You heard it yourself. A good God with good plans who allows bad things? It makes no sense. Why listen to this?

"The Bible is full of people who had to live with challenges. Our good God allowed difficulties. We think of the letter to the Hebrews. Many great stories of faith. Moses. Who remembers the story of Moses?"

Many children raised their hands. I did not. I did remember the story, but I was too engrossed in what he was saying to want to break any connection by moving.

"He believed God, and the waters parted. That is a great story. And sometimes we want God only to be like that all the time. To be a God who makes our lives the way we want them to be. To be delivered from every sort of trouble immediately and to pass through without harm."

He stopped. Looked out at us. Looked at me in particular. He smiled with the gentle smile men of God have when they are carrying out what they are called to do.

"And yet, God allows difficulties. Hebrews also talks about people who loved Jesus but their lives were very difficult. And here, my dear, dear children. Here is what I want you to know. It is not for us to understand why things happen. The God who parted the waters for Moses is the same God who was with Paul when he was shipwrecked and with many others who suffered many trials. He is the same God who was with you before you came to MCF and He is the same God who is with you now. The question I have for you is, are you willing to surrender all to God and allow Him to live His life through you?"

He paused again. I felt the silence. Felt as if every worry and trouble I had ever faced had left me, giving me the opportunity to take in the words of life being spoken to me.

"We wonder, what is the message of God to us? What does God want to say? Does He only want to say, 'Do this. Don't do that'? Or is there something more? The number-one message of God is this: God loves you. God loves you exactly how you are. You are loved without doing anything for Him."

I agreed with him. I could no more influence God to love me than I could convince the stars above to shine down on me.

"Be encouraged not to worry about what you have passed through. Leave the past in God's care. Focus ahead. When you believe in Him and trust in Him you will see marvellous things. It takes great faith to believe God even when things do not make sense."

I thought of all the difficulties in my life. I could not make sense of the events of my past. But then I wondered—did I need to? I was sure that there was a perfect order to the stars above. And I was also sure that I was not capable of understanding what that order was. But whether or not I understood how the stars fit together did not make any difference in how they looked. The stars were beautiful, whether I understood the science behind them or not.

Still, I wondered how God could use the events in my life for good. How could this possibly happen?

It can't. Those things cannot be redeemed.

But they can. You just need to turn to Jesus. Even though things don't make sense.

The cross is supposed to make sense; the problem is that it doesn't. How could it? God is a God who plays favourites. You heard it yourself. He saved Moses, but He did not save others.

The disciples felt confused when Jesus died, didn't they? They could not understand. Not even one of them. But after the resurrection they did come to understand. And they saw that in everything God had a purpose.

"God loves you and accepts you just as you are. That's love. Real love. Yet each of us has sinned. Our sins separate us from God. Deep down inside, every one of us knows this. We have stolen. We have had evil thoughts. The Bible says that we have all sinned. We were even born into sin. And yet, God sent Jesus to take all your sins on Him. He died for you. He died in your place. He took the punishment you and I deserved onto Himself. The Bible says, 'He Himself bore our sins in His body on the cross, so that we might die to sin and live to righteousness; for by His wounds you were healed.' And God, through the power of the Holy Spirit, raised Jesus from the dead. God made it possible for you to have the life of Jesus. Does this sound good? It is good. It is amazing. But if knowing this is all that you have, then it is not enough."

He understood me perfectly. He was right. I did know this. I knew all of it. But something was missing.

Something very, very important was missing.

"The Bible also says that as many as received Him, to them He gave the right to be children of God—those who believe in His name. Let me ask you this question: how many of you have Daddy Mulli as your daddy?"

More hands went up.

Not mine. I was still unable to lift my hands.

"All of you. And how did that happen? Daddy Mulli came to you in your situation and offered you a chance to come here. To MCF. And our God in heaven is coming to each of you tonight. He wants you to live with Him. And He wants to live His life through you right now. Will you allow Him? Will you ask forgiveness for your sins? Will you turn your life over to God? Will you accept His love for you? Will you let everything go and put your faith, your trust, in Jesus alone?"

Yes, there were hurts. Yes, there were questions. Yes, there was confusion. But I wanted to give it all to Jesus. Without having everything in my life resolved, I believed I could have peace at the cross.

"The Bible says to repent and believe the gospel. What is that word *repent*? We need to turn from our old ways. We need to lay our whole lives at the foot of the cross and ask forgiveness. We cannot reach God. It is impossible. Like a creek or a river that is too far for us to jump over. But with God, all things are possible. The gospel is that Jesus took your place and offers you His life. God is reaching out to you to make you His child. His cross is like a bridge from God to you."

I thought of the bridge I crossed every day. I remembered the creaking sound it made when I passed over it. After crossing the bridge, I often glanced at Jacob's Well, a reminder of the water that wasn't supposed to be there.

"To believe means to put your trust in what God has promised. Hearing the promises of eternal life is not enough. Each of us must repent and believe. We must believe—we must put our trust in God. And when we do, God by His grace grants us His life. His eternal life. No condemnation. No fear. No punishment. If you would like to receive Jesus and to cross over from death to life, I invite you to come to the front."

This is it. Now is the time.

This is nothing. What is walking to the front going to do? Just wait a few moments, and soon this will all be over.

This is what I am meant to do. To become a child of God.

You have heard all these stories before. What difference does tonight make?

I heard them. But did I really understand them?

Of course. You are brilliant. You are on your way to becoming a doctor. You understand them perfectly.

But all of this is not about singing or a bed or even being part of a large family. This ...

This what?

This ...

What?

This is all about being in a relationship with Jesus.

You are reaching. You are making much too much out of this.

I do not understand why things happened. But I no longer need to. I know that my sins are forgiven. I am Daddy Mulli's child on earth. Now I want to be God's child in heaven.

Stay in your seat. You don't want to embarrass yourself.

Now is the time.

Now is nothing.

And I will dwell in the house of the Lord forever.
Stay in your seat.

I stood up. I felt a strength come over me I had not known before. I quietly moved to the end of the aisle. People edged back in their seats to make way for me. I took my first step on the dirt ground of the middle aisle. I thought of Jesus as He carried His cross. He took all those steps for me. And now here I was all these years later taking steps to meet Him.

I reached the front where other children had gathered. The pastor prayed for us. Then I prayed.

Dear God, You see my whole life. You love me. I ask You to forgive me. I turn everything over to You. Please change my life. I repent and I believe in You. I put my faith and my trust only in You. Nothing else. I ask You to make me Your child. I leave everything in Your hands. Help me to thank You for everything. And help me to know that You have a plan for me, whatever happens.

In that moment, I felt peace. Like I could sail on a calm ocean despite whatever storm I had just been through. I had known God's love. I had sensed it when I was singing. But now I knew what it meant for Him to live inside me. The two of us together as one, like a choir made up of many members who sang and danced as a single person.

Strange, even though I did not have answers for the troubles in my life, they now took on new meaning. I saw them in a different light. Instead of a forest of confusion, they became like glass reflecting light through them.

It felt like a spring of water flowed out from me, including all the places where there was once pain. For the first time, I could look to the future without seeing the past.

I was a Mully child because Daddy had adopted me into his family. Now I was a child of God because my Father in heaven had adopted me into His family.

The pastor prayed again. He gave me words of encouragement. Then he dismissed us.

Isabella came to the front to see me. I understood her smile now.

"It is a great day for you," she said. "Now we are sisters for eternity."

She hugged me, and I felt myself smile the biggest smile I ever had since coming to MCF. And then, just as quickly as it came, it subsided again. Isabella had done so much for me.

"Thank you," I said as I pulled back.

She raised her eyebrows a split second, then shrugged her shoulders. We talked awhile under the canopy of stars above. We laughed. We listened. It felt different.

We said good night, and I went to my dorm and she to hers.

• • •

I sang a song with the children, prayed with them, helped them into bed, and tucked them in. I clicked off the lights. Going to bed felt different for me that night. I slid into my bunk and glanced outside through the window. The stars shone the brightest I had ever seen.

I knew Jesus. I did not just know *about* Him. I knew Him personally. In my heart. In my soul. In my spirit.

And He knew me.

Peace was not a feeling. It was a person.

I crawled under the covers and thought about my new relationship with Jesus.

I had someone who would stick closer than anyone else. Someone who parted the waters of all my questions in life. Someone who led me safely on dry ground to the other side.

I had the comfort of being a child of God.

I had the peace of knowing I was who I was created to be.

And the assurance of knowing I would dwell in the house of the Lord forever.

CHAPTER
twenty

I looked out at the hundreds of people from the surrounding community who had gathered on our property. Word had gone out that MCF would be providing free medical care to anyone who came, and the response was predictably incredible. In the Ndalani region, you can rely on a centuries-old method of communication for getting the word out. You tell as many people as you can, and they in turn spread the word face to face with those whom they know. And on and on it goes without any fear of the chain being broken. Good news is impossible to keep to yourself.

I saw elderly people wearing old dusty clothes sitting on the ground. Younger children who should have been running around enjoying the early morning hours were instead holding their mothers' hands, their eyes and faces tired from having to combat whatever was ailing them. Seeing such a massive crowd caused me to hold my breath. I did not look long—I was sure I would have broken down and cried had I stared longer. So many people. So much need. I wished I could reach out my hand and heal every one of them.

I hurried to my post at the doctors' station. I helped each day that week at the MCF medical mission. Doctors, nurses, and other volunteers journeyed from overseas to care for the medical needs of MCF children and members of the community. The need was so desperate that people often had to walk three hours, only to stand in a long line.

I met with patients when they first arrived to learn of their ailments and reported them to the medical personnel. Then I translated between doctor and patient as they discussed the illness and the treatments. I felt privileged to be able to bridge the gap between doctor and patient. It gave me a chance to feel what it would be like to give medical advice. I learned so much about how doctors ask questions and diagnose problems. I admired how their minds worked. How they analyzed and solved problems.

After the patients had met with the medical team, I provided them with the prescribed medication. After the medical work was completed, I spent time with the patients, allowing the doctors and nurses time to concentrate on their activities. I loved listening to the patients. I loved hearing their stories, encouraging them, and praying with them. Many had mental, emotional, or relational problems in addition to their medical issues. Their minds and hearts needed healing as much as their bodies did. For all of us at MCF it was important to offer to minister to the entire person. Even if the patient just came for physical help.

The days were long. People who serve at MCF understand this as normal. We started at six in the morning and worked right through until ten in the evening. We looked after hundreds and hundreds of people. Each morning we saw a sea of people arrive on the grounds and wait for help. And each night when I came home to my bed, I found myself barely able to say a prayer before collapsing asleep.

It felt good to serve. I felt the honour that comes with an exhausted body and a full heart. When we closed the clinic on the last day, I felt rejuvenated, like I had been given an injection of energy. I watched as the last group of people began their long walk home. I thought about the incredible hurt in the world and the responsibility I had to do the best I could to help. Yes, there were many more who needed to be reached. But at times like these, I chose to focus on the many we were able to reach, the ones to whom we could show the love of Jesus.

I closed the door of the clinic, having spent the day cleaning up after everyone left. I felt a combination of gratitude and sadness. I missed the patients already. I missed the little children. I missed seeing the stream of people walking to and from the clinic. I missed helping in a practical way. I missed spending time with them.

"Ah, Hannah. How are you doing?"

His words felt like a hug. I felt a calm come over me, the way I always did when I heard him. I turned around. His gentle smile was unmistakable, his never-ending joy contagious. And his childlike love captivating.

"I am well, Daddy."

Daddy Mulli walked up to me. His gentle demeanour felt like the warmth of the sun at the exact time of day when it reaches its ideal temperature.

"What a wonderful week! Wow! I tell you, there were so many people who were helped. Many, many people coming from all directions. All over. Many places. They had to walk a long way. And you, Hannah, you gave of your time and your talents to help make this possible."

"It was a good medical mission, Daddy."

"Very good. Amazing! The power of God was really at work here. All the volunteers. You all did so well. You woke up so early. And you worked hard all day. And you went to bed very late in the evening. I can't even imagine how hard you all worked. Really, it's a miracle."

"Thank you for letting me work here."

"Of course! How could I not? A wonderful person like you wanting to serve. It is like a plane taking off, heading high into the sky."

He laughed so hard. I laughed with him. He had such energy. Such optimism. And then he became quiet—the way he did whenever he wanted to share something deep. Something profound.

"You made a big decision last week to follow Jesus," he said. "I am very proud of you. Nothing makes me happier than to know God is now your heavenly Father."

"Thank you, Daddy."

"And He will accomplish His will through you," he said. "You have a wonderful, gentle spirit with a deep compassion for people. You have this. You do. Nobody told you that you had to talk to the people after they received their medical help. But you did. From your heart. You went and talked and listened to people share about their problems. Many people have no one to talk to. But you made yourself available. You could have said, 'I want to take a break. It's been very long and very hot, and I want to go.' And could have left and gone somewhere to relax. But you did not. You, out of your own heart, you listened and you served. And God will make you a blessing to many people. You see, He has already made you into a blessing to people this entire week."

I felt the spirit with which he said those words. I thought about the week. About the people.

"Do you ever have worry if God will provide enough help?" I asked. "There are so many people. So much need."

He noticed that I was looking slightly into the sun. He stepped to the side so that my gaze was shielded by the shade of the trees.

"It is a good question. Our job is to be faithful. And God's job is to provide as He sees fit and when He sees fit. It is not for us to worry. Jesus says, 'Look at the birds of the air, that they do not sow, nor reap nor gather into barns, and yet your heavenly Father feeds them.' Jesus tells us to seek first His kingdom and His righteousness. And that is what I am doing. I seek after Him. It is up to God to deliver the rest. And He will do so faithfully."

Daddy helped me better understand that God was in control. Even though we could not reach everyone, we could reach the ones we could and leave the rest in God's care.

"Do you have a moment to talk?" he continued. "There is something I would like to share with you," he said.

"Of course."

"You are sure? You have time? It is okay?"

The real question was whether *he* had any time. If it fit *his* schedule to talk. It wasn't a question of whether I had the time. Though Daddy did not see it this way. In his mind, he did not presume that any of his children would have time to speak with him. So he always asked. Never one to assume. Never one to intrude. I smiled and nodded.

We crossed the bridge, passed Jacob's Well, and walked together to the large house undergoing construction. It was originally intended many years earlier to be his eventual retirement home. But he had given up his retirement. Along with everything else. We sat down on wooden chairs under the protection of the second floor being built.

"You have put your trust in Jesus," he said. "And I want to encourage you in your walk of faith. Even as we plant trees here at MCF and we see so many of them growing and changing this area, so God wants you to grow in your life with Jesus. And this happens as we read our Bible, as we pray, and as we obey Jesus in everything we do. Just like the tree needs water and sunlight all the time, so we need to stay focused on Jesus. This is how Jesus lives His life in us and through us."

"Thank you for giving me the Bible. It really helps me to spend time with God." He nodded in his humble, gentle way. "I want to thank you," I continued. "I have received everything here. A new family. A new home. And you showed me the way of eternal life in Christ. You have done so much; I really could never thank you enough."

I had never seen him this quiet before. He waited in the silence, and to me it seemed like something I had said had touched him. I found this comforting. Perhaps in some small way I could offer him a glass of water in exchange for the ocean he had given me.

"Thank you," he whispered. Then he smiled. "So, I would like to ask you, do you have a favourite tree here at MCF?" he asked.

I laughed. "Well, I actually have two. Is it okay to have two favourites?"

"Yes, it is fine."

"My favourites are mango and banana."

"Very good. Yes, those are wonderful fruits. I love them too."

"Which is your favourite?"

"Me?"

"Yes, you. Which is your favourite tree?"

"Can I really tell you?" Daddy asked.

I raised my eyebrows to say yes.

"Well. I would have to say ... all of them."

We both exploded in laughter. My stomach shook. My smile was so wide, I felt the skin on my face stretch.

"That is a good favourite to have," I said. I exhaled and tried to catch my breath.

Daddy took in a deep breath. "You know, each of these fruit trees are planted and grown not just so they can look nice but so they can be of benefit to others. You understand?"

I shifted my weight in my chair. I focused on his deep brown eyes.

"Jesus says to us, 'freely you received, freely give.' I want to encourage you to continue to be someone who gives. Just like you gave of your time this week. Just like the tree gives fruit to everyone and not for itself. You might wonder, 'What does that mean, to give? Is it to do what I do by giving my resources to help others?' Yes, it is that. We need to share. Even as little children we are taught to share. And as we get older, we need to remember that we are called to share what we have with other people. But we need to ask ourselves what our motivation is to share."

I heard a vehicle driving up in the distance. I saw a group returning from MCF Yatta. A dog barked nearby. Daddy's eyes stayed on me.

"Jesus taught us to love our neighbour. This is to be our motivation. Sometimes we can give out of guilt. We feel we are supposed to give, and so we do it with a closed heart. But true followers of Jesus will give because they love the person they are giving to. And this is my encouragement to you. As you study to become a doctor, as you work so hard for this dream, that you will always be motivated out of a deep love for people. Remember, perfect love casts out fear. And when you have that love for other people, you can really give with all your heart."

I wanted to be that kind of person. I wanted to be the way Daddy was with all of his generosity. To give. To love. With such genuineness.

The way life was intended.

The entire MCF vision was so incredible to me. It was a place of refuge, of miracles, and of staggering accomplishment. Yet, when I spoke with Daddy Mulli, it all became so simple. A humble man, trusting our Almighty God, and loving everyone with whom he came into contact.

What more could I ask for in my own life?

"Thank you, Daddy."

"Many times we think that we have to continually look out for ourselves. But God will look after us. He will look after you. Even me—when I had all my wealth, when I began to give it all away—people thought I was really crazy. They thought, what is this man doing? Why is he acting this way? He has gone mad. Completely. But the love I have for each of you motivated me to give everything away." He waited a moment for a group to pass by. When it became quiet again he continued. "I would like to ask you a question."

I nodded. "All right."

"Look around you here. What do you think is more important? For me to have kept my hold on my way of life? Or to have given up everything to love people and give of myself to them?"

A group of younger children laughed as they hurried past us to the play area.

"I see how the love of God in you has impacted so many people," I said. "Including me."

"And God will impact people through you as well."

Did he just say that? In an instant, his words completely enveloped me. How did he do that, exactly? It was like it wasn't even him talking. Like God was talking through him. To me. Right here. Could God really work through me to impact people?

"I hope so."

"He will. Even when you least expect it. God works His will out all the time. Especially in ways we do not immediately understand."

"Thank you for speaking with me," I said.

"Of course. Thank you," he said as he smiled with a laugh. "So I hope you will have a wonderful rest of your day."

"You too." I laughed as well. It was impossible to do anything else around him.

He smiled. "And remember, the mangos are just about in season. I cannot wait. Wow! They will taste so good!"

He stood up. And as he left I thought about his words. *And God will impact people through you as well.*

I wondered if that was actually possible.

• • •

A number of months later, we faced a drought in Ndalani and in the surrounding region. We had a storehouse where we kept all the purchased food, like rice and beans and other food. But as you can imagine, a drought that affects MCF also affects the surrounding community. As the drought became worse, and as our crops did not provide the yield we hoped for, and as the food in our storehouse decreased, we were faced with the real possibility of not having enough to eat. Our neighbours faced the same challenge.

And then something strange happened.

Daddy Mulli took all the food out of our storehouse and gave it to the community around us. That left us with nothing. We had no food and no money to buy it with.

Hundreds upon hundreds of us children had nothing. Not so much as one bean was left in the storehouse to feed us.

I watched him as he walked among the community people who had gathered on our property. "Have you had enough to eat?" he asked. They nodded. He stopped and talk with whoever needed a listening ear. Yes, he gave. But, true to his word, he loved them. He did not simply look at people. He had that gift of looking into people.

When we were left with nothing, Daddy prayed. And soon after, a phone call came, and then a large truck pulled up and off-loaded an incredible amount of food. The workers were astonished.

Daddy Mulli was happy. But not amazed. It was as if he knew what was going to happen.

I wondered how he could face such a challenge—such a disaster, really—with such confidence.

And it filled me with the most incredible faith I had ever felt.

CHAPTER
twenty-one

I loved the time of the morning just before sunrise. I would sense the quiet of MCF. It felt like everything had a chance to unwind and could remain in a quiet calm before the busyness of the day began. These were special moments for me. In a place that typically had much activity, these early mornings gave me a unique experience to hear the quiet calling of God on my heart. I would stay in my bed and notice the slightest increase in the level of light outside, serving as notification that a new day was just ahead. The warm transition from the darkness of the night began when the first hint of golden rays reflected off Pride Rock high above us. The light rolled down the mountain onto MCF as if God were laying a blanket of protection over us, showing the beauty of our home in what was once a barren land.

Like on many other mornings, I began the day quietly in my bed, not saying or reading or asking for anything. I stayed in the stillness with God. Listening to His silence. Like the sun, His presence covered me and reached inside me, giving me the peace that made me want to stay with Him there forever.

I then read my Bible and prayed for MCF, my siblings, the children in my dorm, and my studies. We heard the bell to wake up, and then everything got started. Encouraging the children to get out of bed. Singing with them. Giving them a hug. Helping them get ready. Taking them to breakfast. Then, getting them off to school. I took a breath as I watched their little legs hurrying off to class. So much fun. So humbling to be part of helping to raise them.

• • •

I looked out at Mully Mountain, fully illuminated in the brightness of the day.

"It is a beautiful morning," I heard behind me. Mommy Mulli's words were followed by her quiet and deep laugh, coming from deep inside her, bringing joy to my heart each time I heard it. Like the way the sun reveals the beauty of MCF hidden in the night, her voice revealed the love and acceptance that filled her heart.

When you have a passport and you enter another county, an official stamps it as proof that they accept you. This is how it felt when I was around Mommy Mulli.

"It is," I replied. I turned to see her standing in the corner, giving a package of maize to one of the kitchen staff.

"Do you have time to help?" she asked.

I nodded.

She picked up a box with one arm and held out her other arm for me to join her. I came beside her, and she wrapped her arm around me. We walked out towards one of the fields.

"Do you like mangos?" she asked with a quizzical expression.

"I do."

"Ah, that is good," she said with another laugh.

I suppose it is possible that there are better places in the world than being with my mommy and daddy. But if there is such a place, I have not yet found it.

We stopped at a mango tree and began to pick the ripened fruit.

"You know how to tell when a mango is ripe?" she asked. I had picked mangos before. I could tell from looking at them which ones were ripe. She picked a red and orange mango and gently pressed her thumb against the middle. "You can squeeze it just a little and then you see that it is not hard." She handed it to me. I pressed my thumbs in, and they sunk in slightly, just the way I expected.

She picked a green mango from the other side of the tree. I expected it to be rock hard. Yet, she pressed her thumb gently against the skin, and it gave in. I must have given a puzzled expression.

"You did not expect this?" she asked.

"No."

"Sometimes we think a mango is only ripe when it is a certain colour or when it looks a certain way. But this is not correct. The skin colour, the way it looks on the outside, is not the way to tell if it is ripe. The sun makes them ripe. You can see that these two mangos look completely different, and yet they are both ripe."

I held both in my hand and felt their soft skin against my palms. The green mango was smaller than the red one. But as I pressed my thumbs against the green one, I could tell it was ripe too.

"They look different?" she asked as we continued picking. We tested each one to make sure it was ripe before pulling it from the tree.

"Yes."

"They are different, yet they are both beautiful. Do you understand?"

She was hinting at something deeper. The message of which escaped me for the moment.

"I am not sure."

"The green mango did not look ripe. But it was ripe. And once you know that it is ripe, once you understand that it is ripe even though it looks green, you begin to see it as beautiful."

I thought about this as I watched her pick a larger mango and place it into the box. She worked with such care and diligence. I heard that many years ago, Daddy and Mommy met for the first time when she was working in a field. Her mother was sick, and Mommy went to work as a young woman in her place for a few days. Daddy was a young man supervising the entire company. He was popular. All the young women knew of him. And yet, of all the women who knew Daddy Mulli, he chose her.

"We are all beautiful before God," she continued. "Sometimes the negative influences of other people make us feel like giving up because we do not look the same on the outside. But we are all created in the image of God. And it takes real courage to reject the world's thinking that beauty is only on the outside. It takes courage to have faith to trust God's definition of beauty."

"Thank you," I whispered.

"You are beautiful, Hannah. You are beautiful because God has made you. Always remember that."

"I will."

She became quiet. She studied me, looking into me with kindness and wisdom.

"You have a gift of being able to connect with people. I see you when you talk to Isabella and to the little children. They are comfortable around you. They feel safe that they can share their heart. That is a precious gift."

I nodded. We finished packing the mangos in the box. She smiled, and we walked back. I glanced back at the tree.

I would not forget it.

• • •

After supper, we went to our evening studies, which we called preps. I reviewed the science lessons from earlier that day and then read ahead to what we would be taking the next day. I found the more I learned on my own in advance of the classroom, the better I understood the concepts. It made class time easier. Because I had studied ahead, when I came to class I was hearing the lesson for the second or even third time. Instead of using the classroom as a place to be introduced to new ideas, I found it a place to fill in the gaps in my understanding from what I had learned the night before.

Afterward I walked with Isabella to choir practice, joking with her on the way. I glanced above to the beautiful stars shining down, filling the night sky with their unique dazzling spectacle. It took my breath away that night, as it did each night.

We opened the door to the choir room. It felt like travelling right into heaven. I sensed the rush of joy and the thrill of being able to spend time worshipping God. We took our places, began shuffling our feet, moved our arms in rhythm, and started singing. I closed my eyes and enjoyed the feeling. I had sometimes wondered how in eternity it would be possible to do something over and over again and not get used to it. But as I sang, it occurred to me that I could do this without end. I could sing and let time disappear forever.

And so we sang in the dark of night.

But in our hearts, it was an eternal sunrise.

CHAPTER
twenty-two

There are times in life when we overcome great challenges and make real progress. But then, if we are not careful, we can retreat and try to make life predictable and comfortable. It is as if we climb a mountain and reach the top; then after the celebration, instead of pressing on to a new goal, something inside us resists another challenge. We think we have been stretched to the limit. And that life of reckless abandon that we once knew, of trusting and listening to God, becomes cloudy, and we fall back to a life of safety.

Daddy Mulli happens to have the ability to spot this complacency in people.

In me, for example.

My studies were going well. I was on my way to becoming a doctor. I enjoyed serving at MCF so much. I loved singing in the choir. I was thrilled with looking after children. Life was challenging enough.

At least that's what I thought.

After an evening devotional, Daddy Mulli asked me to stay behind for a moment.

"Hello, Hannah. How are you?" he asked in his kind tone.

"I am fine, Daddy. And you? How are you?"

"Great. Amazing." He laughed. And as always, when he laughed, I laughed. I challenge anyone not to be happy around him.

"That is good."

"We have much to be thankful for," he said. He was right. We had God. We had food. We had clothing. And we had the wisdom of being content with these.

The last of my brothers and sisters left the devotion area. I heard a group of my brothers in the distance, laughing at a joke someone had told. I felt the cool of the evening, a welcome relief to the heat of the day. I had planned on going to evening study after the devotional. And then talk with my little children before tucking them in for night. It was going to be an evening like any other. Until I heard Daddy Mulli's next words, that is.

"Hannah, I would like you to join the mission team to Tanzania."

That sounded great. I had never been to Tanzania, and I loved the thought of being able to go there.

"All right," I said.

"You will be going with other members of the choir," Daddy said.

So far, so good.

"And, as you know, there are many people in Dar es Salaam who do not know Christ."

My mind started connecting the dots. Mission team. Jesus. I had an idea of what was coming, but there was no way he was going to ask me to—

"I would like for you to go door to door and tell people about Jesus."

The temperature at MCF Ndalani does not get below freezing. It can get cold, but we have never had ice. Yet, I can say with absolute certainty that when Daddy Mulli asked me to speak to people face to face, I froze.

"You are scared."

Scared? Yes, but more than that. Terrified, actually. *I will look after children. I will study every free moment I have to get into medical school. I will sing praises to God all day long. I will travel to the ends of the earth to sing. No problem. But I can't speak with strangers at the best of times, and certainly not about something so intimate, something so important, as my faith. I just can't. I beg you. I beg you from the bottom of my heart. Don't make me speak one-on-one with people.*

I found it difficult to breathe. I swallowed.

"I am scared. Yes," I said.

"Do not be afraid."

I wanted to have the same confidence in me as he had. I wanted to believe. I did. But this just did not fit my personality. I wondered if he had made a mistake in asking me to do this.

I became worried. I worried I would not do well. That I would let Daddy down. That my inability to evangelize would reflect badly on MCF at best and push someone further away from the gospel at worst.

"All right," I said in less than a whisper.

In our culture, it is not polite to disagree with our elders. He knew this. I knew this. Still, he sensed my hesitation, worry, and insecurity.

"Sometimes in life we can have doubts. And when we doubt ourselves, this is actually a good thing. Because it causes us to ask if we are willing to trust God, to be used by Him—especially in places where we do not think we have natural talent."

I thought about having to actually speak with someone. Approaching someone I did not know was a scary thought. I pushed it away. I looked into Daddy's eyes. Overcoming fear becomes easier when you can share it with someone who cares.

"You are sure about choosing me?"

"Oh yes. I am sure. There are two things we must have if we are going to effectively tell people about God. We must love God, and we must love the people we speak to. And Hannah, I know you have both. Are you willing to trust God in this?"

I waited. Thought. Tried to find the faith that seemed to be escaping me. In that moment, I understood the man who said to Jesus, "I do believe; help my unbelief."

I breathed.

"Yes," I said.

"Very good. We start training tomorrow."

• • •

That evening, as I said prayers with the children, I found myself in that place where I actually hoped they would pray for me instead. Each day, I encouraged the children to pray, to trust God, to move forward with

Him in faith. Who was I to think that their struggles were any easier than mine? I looked into their precious faces as we sat together in a circle. They all folded their hands and bowed their heads. I wished I had the same faith they did.

"Dear God," I prayed. "Thank You for loving us. We love You, too. You made us. And You gave us such a wonderful home here at MCF. I pray You will help us trust You in everything. In Jesus' name. Amen."

We gave hugs, and after the children settled into their beds, I crawled into mine. I wanted to fall asleep, wanted to let the problems of the day go. But I felt my mind spinning. I felt unable to settle down.

I am not the right person to do this.

That's right. You are totally wrong for this.

I am not an outgoing person.

Exactly. You are quiet and keep to yourself. To be useful in sharing Jesus, you must be a loud and outgoing person. You will be a total failure in trying to reach anyone.

But Daddy said to trust God.

Forget what Daddy said. He has made a terrible mistake in choosing you.

But he wasn't wrong in rescuing me. Why would he be wrong now?

I turned over on my side, hoping it would help to clear my mind and my heart.

Please, God. Why am I so worried? I have given my testimony, and I have sung in front of many people. Why does sharing about You scare me so much? I feel terrible for feeling this way.

When you were with Mommy Esther at the mango tree, what did I teach you?

That I am beautiful.

This is the truth. I took great care in planning everything about you. I spent a lot of time in crafting every part of you. Keep your eyes on Me, and don't worry about the results. How does that sound?

It sounds good.

I felt a sudden change in my thinking. Yes, it was true that I was a quieter person. That was a fact. But I was wrong about what that fact meant. God could use a quiet person like me just as much as He could use a louder person. Telling others about Jesus did not depend on my ability.

It depended on God's ability. And Daddy was right. I did love people. I loved them very much.

I closed my eyes and drifted off.

And wondered what it would be like to have this adventure in Tanzania.

• • •

We spent a lot of time as a team praying for the mission to Tanzania. With each meeting, we sensed an increasing confidence that God was in control, that this mission was His mission, that He had called us together be His representatives. We asked God to prepare in advance the hearts of people we would be meeting. And we prayed that He would work to save people who did not yet know Him.

Daddy Mulli often came to our evening meetings. We gathered in one of the senior high classrooms, where he offered us words of encouragement.

"When you are a missionary, you need to be courageous. Fear and evangelism can never go together. It takes courage to talk to someone about Jesus. In Tanzania, you will meet a lot of people. Many, many people from many different places. They will have different backgrounds than you. They will challenge you in what you are doing. In what you are saying. Remember, when you are talking about God, be confident. You are talking about the real thing. You are not lying. You speak the truth. Every person is designed by God and for God. You have what they need. And when you speak the truth in love, God will change lives."

I felt a stirring in my heart, a confidence building. I was ready now more than ever to get on that bus. We would be leaving early the next morning. But if I could have, I would have gone right then and there.

"He will work through each one of you."

I glanced around the room at my brothers and sisters. We were a group of former orphans, street children, or children from homes where we could no longer be looked after. We had been ignored by so many people, written off as an impossible problem. Yet God in His goodness was ready to use us as missionaries in a different country.

"It does not matter if you have been doing this for many years or if this is your first time. God will be with you. And as you trust in Him, the evil one will not be able to harm you."

Daddy Mulli prayed over us. He wished us well. I wanted him to come along, but his many responsibilities prevented him from coming on the journey with us.

So it would be that much more exciting to bring him the news of our journey when we returned. It made me wonder what that news would be. Especially considering we were about to go out and live it.

That evening before going to my dormitory I went to meet Zemira at the evening devotional area. We had agreed to meet the night before I left. Strange for both of us. It would be the first time we would ever be apart.

She had arrived first. She sat on the bench looking at the direction of the path leading up from the bridge in the direction I would be coming. The moment our eyes met, she smiled. The way she smiled indicated to me that she was trying hard to cover up her sorrow.

And I wondered if I was, too.

We gave each other a hug. I sat down next to her. Both of us tried to look brave. Both of us failed.

"I am going to miss you," Zemira said.

"I am going to miss you too." I put my left arm around her shoulder.

"I will be praying for you," she said.

"Thank you. I will pray for you too."

She was quiet a moment. I knew what was coming.

"I will pray that you make it back safe and sound."

"It will be all right," I said.

We were both older now, and we knew what that meant. What that really meant. It wasn't sugar-coating to live in a pretend world where we said nice things and had the luxury of living a fairy-tale existence where our wishes would always become reality. We had lived reality. We knew that life does not always work out the way you want it to. But since coming to MCF, we had discovered that in God all things did work out. Either here, or there. And in that sense, it really would be all right.

She nodded. She needed more.

"Hey," I said. She looked up at me. "You need to trust. All right?" She nodded again. Yes, there was a massive family now. Hundreds of us. But with blood, it was down to the two of us. And leaving for the first time brought that sense back to us. So I tried to reassure her. "We have a big family. So remember, our family is really everyone who believes on the

Lord Jesus Christ. And I know all of you will be praying for us every day. And we will be praying for you."

She nodded. I understood what this meant, even if anyone else could not. I hugged her with both arms. I could not hear it, but I sensed she was crying.

"Everything will be fine," I whispered. "And when I come back we will go for a long walk together. How does that sound?"

I pulled back. She wiped her tears away.

"It sounds good. Have a fun time."

"I will."

"It is very neat. That you get to go. I am proud of you."

"I am proud of you too. Lala salama," I said, wishing her a good night.

"Lala salama," she said.

We stood to our feet. We walked together part of the way and then broke apart for her to go to her dorm and me to mine.

"Where will we go for a walk?" she called out to me.

"Wherever you like. That will be your job. To decide on a place."

She raised her eyebrows.

I did too.

• • •

As was our custom, we woke the next morning before sunrise. We gathered outside the bus, still half-asleep. Daddy once owned many companies, and one of them was a bus company called MullyWays. Now, all these years later, after he had sold his businesses, he was transporting me—a quiet yet confident-in-the-Lord missionary—on his bus.

Daddy and Mommy hugged us and prayed for us before we stepped on. I so admired their humble love for each other. For us. For God. A group including Zemira had gotten up early as well to see us off. I took my seat at a window. I watched them waving to us.

We turned onto the highway. Some of the children were already fast asleep. It would take us a day to get there, which would be lots of time to spend praying for the people we would encounter.

• • •

The bus ride to Dar es Salaam was bumpy and fun. We told jokes, read our Bibles, and sang a lot of songs. One person, sometimes me, would start singing, and then the entire bus would join in. I loved the sound of singing on the bus. It sounded so full in the enclosed space—something so different from the open air or even the classroom settings we were used to. After every song we felt the last note reverberate. I imagined what it must have been like for God to look down and see our humble bus travelling down the highway while we sang praises to Him. I am sure He enjoyed it. I planned to ask Him about it when I saw Him.

When I thought to myself of how much time Daddy made for us at MCF, I sometimes wondered how God would make time for the many millions and millions of people there would be in heaven. I didn't know how He would do it, exactly, but somehow I felt that God would be able to make enough time for each of us.

We were supposed to have reached Dar es Salaam in 12 hours. But a car accident on the highway had blocked the road for many hours. We had not seen the accident occur, but we prayed for whoever was involved in it nonetheless. Our team had to spend the night in the town of Mombo in Tanzania. And it served as a lesson to me that we need to surrender our plans to God. That He works according to His schedule. The next morning, we continued our journey.

• • •

As we approached Dar es Salaam, the excitement I thought I was going to feel was replaced with a deep sense of sorrow. I felt the weight of suffering on me. I saw row after row of rusty brown roofs. It was as if someone had taken a large bucket of old paint and splashed it over the entire area as far as I could see, giving it a consistent depressing look.

We drove closer, and I saw children playing in dirty water. Barefoot. Their clothes old and torn. Some women sat outside the doors of their shacks. Men walked down the street, shuffling like they had been on their feet a very long time. Everyone looked exhausted, the heat of the day and the pressures of life taking their revenge on them. The outward state of their rotting homes mirrored the condition of their souls. Everything looked crammed together as if two bulldozers had lined up to jam the already crowded houses even closer together.

Our bus became quiet. We had seen slums before. Most of us had lived in them. But every time we saw poverty—real, desperate poverty—it reminded us of how desperate each of us once was. I thought about the thousands—millions—of children who were in slums like this one, suffering from poverty, fear, and hopelessness. It made me wonder why I was chosen to be part of MCF. Yet more than that, it caused me to struggle with the responsibility I had, as one who was rescued, to do my part to change the lives of others. Any time any of us was in a slum, it reminded us that without outside intervention we would have just as easily been those precious people on the other side of the window. And in that moment, I thought to myself that I could just as easily have been born here instead.

The metal roofs of the shacks spread out in every direction, in no apparent order. The slum, as far as I could see, was a complicated maze of disorganized streets and rickety buildings. It felt like I could walk in there and get lost in an endless series of twists and turns.

A stream of greenish water ran alongside a row of shacks. I made a mental note to avoid walking near it. I saw men building a mud wall of a home. They had set up large branches to serve as framing and packed in a combination of stones and mud to complete the wall.

A group of women wearing colourful dresses—a bright red one stood out to me—washed clothes using plastic buckets of blue, red, green, and orange. They hung their clothes on a washing line, creating a flash of colours in the bright sun. Little children played near the women, fulfilling the ongoing African tradition of having children alongside their mothers even when they are working.

The odd green bush tried to grow along the banks of the stream, as if to show that the slightest sliver of hope for regeneration might still exist. I saw an old man standing beside a young boy, both of them looking out at a creek littered full of old plastic bags. As I watched the two of them, it made me think that without a drastic change that young boy would end up the same age as that old man and be looking at the same creek someday without having had a chance at something different. It saddened me to think that someone so young was already on a predetermined course.

One that needed to be changed.

I hurt for the people. I felt their pain. It was as if an intravenous line had been hooked up so what was going on inside of them was somehow transferred into me. I felt their drudgery. Their struggle to survive. Their frustration over wanting to get ahead but feeling themselves continually falling further behind. Yet still they struggled, making the best of a desperate situation.

Our bus turned a corner. I looked into the eyes of the people who gazed up at us. Their expressions were evidence that they had long since given up on the possibility of their lives improving. To me it seemed they had resolved themselves that the best they could do was to hang on and live each day, hoping there would be a tomorrow. I sensed that they placed incredible expectation on us. No outsider ever came to a slum to receive. They came to give. So the people in the slum were desperate for our attention. Desperate for us to deliver on whatever promise we would be making to them. I felt the pressure mounting and reminded myself, as we learned in our preparation time, that the battle belonged to the Lord.

The bus stopped at our hostel. The door opened. We gathered our small bags and moved to the front.

When I stepped off the bus, an unbearable blast of heat attacked me. It felt like an oven door had been opened right in front of us. As Kenyans, we are used to heat. But the heat here was far more intense. The temperature was made all the worse by the depressing condition of the people and buildings we had just seen. I took in a breath. I felt the blistering air in my lungs. I coughed.

We settled in at the hostel and got ready for our first event.

It was time to begin.

CHAPTER
twenty-three

None of us knew what to expect.

It was a new country. A new city. New people, many of whom did not have a Christian background. In the slum in Mbagala, I saw many shacks that served as houses cramped together. In the distance, a market area featured many small shops for people to buy food, clothing, and electronics. Children wearing green uniforms entered a small school. All around us, I saw much garbage—on the ground where we walked, on the banks of the streams, covering entire fields, everywhere. Garbage served as a sign that people were so overcome with their daily burdens that they did not have any time or energy to keep everything clean.

We had organized in advance to work with the local churches. Representatives from those churches came to help us. I felt an immediate connection with them, our faith uniting us.

A crowd began to arrive as we set up tables in a clearing. Had this been a wealthy neighbourhood, the area might have been referred to as a park. But there were no parks here, so we set up in a similar style as we did for our slum outreaches in Kenya. Our goal was to offer people spiritual and physical food. A meeting like ours provided a place for people to have a change in their daily routine.

And a change in their eternity too, we hoped.

Our MCF team stood out with our bright orange T-shirts. They displayed our MCF crest—a brown cross bearing the globe and the letters *MCF* with our motto "Saving Children's Lives" beneath it. I felt proud and honoured to wear it, counting it a privilege to be there to share with people.

We had washed our faces. Set our hair. Compared with the exhausted expressions and downtrodden eyes of our guests, there was reason for them to be curious why we came. Despite them being strangers, they seemed like long-lost friends. I smiled at them. Some smiled back. I saw in their eyes that, like drillers searching for long-lost water, their attempts to find a spiritual well had run dry. They had done what they could but had come up empty; and they lacked the outer prosperity to mask their inner poverty.

I saw the look of exasperation that comes with not being able to solve problems or to get ahead. They seemed burdened by the weight of being in a never-ending cycle of poverty. They were surviving. Day to day. In some cases hour by hour. The expressions on their faces exemplified lives filled to overflowing with trouble. Desperation makes every unbearable thing that much more unbearable.

People in slums worked exhausting hours. It was not uncommon for people to walk two hours to work, put in a twelve-hour day, and then walk two hours to return home. They couldn't take the bus, because it would cost them two hours' wages to pay for a one-way ride. They would work these long days for six days a week. Sometimes seven. And if they did not want to do their job, no problem—there were dozens of people lined up waiting to take their place.

After a difficult day of work, they returned to their home life, or perhaps home *existence* would be a better description. It was difficult, if not impossible, for most people to own their own slum dwelling. The shacks in many slums were owned by landlords. The expression *slum landlord* was literally fitting in these cases. After paying for rent, food, and clothing, they had little or no money at the end of the month. There was no welfare system and no old age security. This endless cycle of existing to survive, without any chance of life getting better, plagued people with hopelessness. Many had given up. Some had tried all kinds of ways to make life easier. But they came to the realization that they didn't have what they needed to succeed.

And they didn't know where to find it.

Which is why we were there.

I sang the lead part in our choir. We danced and clapped. The crowd grew, as it also would in Kenya, with the sound of singing. Some people talked with each other. Shifted in their seats on the ground. Despite feeling tired from the heat before the event, I found renewed energy. Daddy Mulli taught us to smile and rely on the joy of the Lord whenever we presented. He told us it didn't matter if there was one person in attendance or hundreds. What mattered was that we shared our hope in Jesus with whomever He had brought. Regardless of how a person might look on the outside, God is at work in the person's heart.

Pastor Josiah stepped up to preach. I always found his speaking effortless and convicting, something I was sure he learned from Daddy Mulli. I admired Pastor Josiah's humility. It made him and others in leadership at MCF so approachable. I found something so reassuring about people like him who depend on God in every circumstance.

When he began to speak, a hush fell over the crowd. A once restless group suddenly grew still, like a stormy lake that in an instant becomes calm. Standing in the slum, under the sweltering and merciless heat, when I looked out at the people I found it staggering to think that here in this slum so many people's eternity stood at stake.

Pastor Josiah presented the gospel. Many gave their lives to Jesus. I watched in amazement as people came forward. It reminded me of what Daddy Mulli told us. *Every person is designed by God and for God. You have what they need. And when you speak the truth in love, God will change lives.*

Here in the poorest area of Dar es Salaam, God used our humble team from Kenya to bring the Good News. And the longer I looked, the more I felt like we had little, if anything, to do with it.

We handed out Bibles and other food—mostly bread and maize flour—and offered to connect people with local churches.

"It is a good start to the day," Pastor Josiah said after we handed out food to the last person in line.

"An excellent start," I said with a smile. Looking out at the crowd eating the food we provided reminded me of the community people we would feed at MCF. God in Kenya was the same God who saved people here. It reinforced for me that the God of the Bible is the same yesterday, today, and forever.

"Once you have finished your lunch we will go door to door. How does that sound?"

My heart jumped at his words. I did my best to refuse to listen to the fear knocking with such force at my door.

Don't risk it! Let the others go. Just stay behind. You don't want to make a mistake.

But I agreed to go. Our God had brought us this far.

"It sounds good," I said.

And it made me curious as to what He had in store next.

• • •

We left the open area and walked into the maze of winding streets. In most larger cities, the roads are laid out in a grid. Slums don't usually work that way. When we drove into the slum the roads felt like a dizzying and haphazard system. And walking around inside the slum felt all the more disorientating. The roads twisted and turned, led to dead ends, circled around to where you were before. The slum layout felt as confusing as the lives of the people in it. The smell of waste filled the air, made all the worse by the stifling heat. My eyes began to tear in reaction to the pungent odour. It was impossible to escape. I did not know whether it was better to breathe in through my nose or my mouth.

The narrow road felt all the more cramped because of the unending rows of tattered, rusted metal shacks that stretched out forever on either side. Small children stopped and watched us with curious eyes. Their smiles deep, shy, and cautious. Their precious hearts still content with having a mother and perhaps also a father in their lives. I smiled and waved at them. They giggled and waved back.

Pastor Josiah approached a set of shacks. He approached it with total confidence. Without hesitating he knocked on the sheet metal doors. When they opened, he would greet the people and ask if they knew Jesus. Many closed the door. Some said they were Muslim. Others said they had a Christian background yet did not want to trust only in Jesus. They claimed they had a set of rules to follow so they could earn their way into heaven. Pastor Josiah listened with kindness. Instead of directly telling them they were wrong, he shared verses from the Bible that show we must be born again and that salvation is found in Jesus Christ alone.

That upset many people, and we were often told to leave. As we were shooed away and began walking to the next home, I felt a combination of sadness and confusion. Sadness because they had turned their back on Jesus in favour of their own religion. And confusion over how someone could be shown the truth right in front of them but not recognize it.

We approached numerous other homes. Some people accepted Christ. That was truly exhilarating. Was there anything better than people having their name written in God's book of life?

I felt comfortable being the quiet girl at the back listening and silently praying for the people in each house we approached. But as we stepped back onto the road after an unsuccessful attempt at a home, Pastor Josiah turned to me.

"It's your turn to knock on the next door," he said.

I felt my pulse quicken.

When you are a missionary, you need to be courageous.

Fear not, for I am with you.

"All right."

I saw a home across the street. I knew the longer I waited, the harder it would get. So instead of wishing for a better time that would not come, I crossed the street.

I heard African music with its lighthearted and funky beat playing in the distance. It grew quieter as I approached the rusty brown door. I noticed a window beside it. No glass, of course. Just bars and shutters. I gathered my courage, praying silently. I lifted my hand.

I knocked.

Admittedly, it was a quiet knock. Too quiet. I waited.

The group waited.

Perhaps no one was home. Resisting the urge to quit, I knocked again, louder this time. I heard feet shuffling to the door. A hinged clicked. The door opened.

A woman, about the age my mother would have been, looked at me from the doorframe.

"Hello," I began. And that was as far as I got.

"No Jesus!"

Apparently, news travelled fast here too. She slammed the door in my face. It rattled. The construction was so poor, I thought the whole front of the shack was going to fall down right then and there, creating an opening into her home and giving me a second chance.

And her.

I exhaled. I heard the music again.

"Don't be discouraged," Pastor Josiah said. "Let's try again."

We walked a little farther, and I saw an older woman sitting on a chair outside her hut. Two little boys and a little girl played around her. She looked out across the street at nothing in particular, the way people do when the pressures of life have become too great and the best relief is found not in distractions but in solitude.

She heard us approaching and turned her attention to us. Her gaze changed. She smiled with the kind of smile that indicated she had learned the secret of choosing her attitude despite her circumstances, as difficult as they were.

"Can I help you?" she asked.

That was a welcome surprise. I had expected to be the one to start the conversation.

"I am Hannah. I—"

"I am pleased to meet you. My name is Kyesi," she said, her Kenyan-Tanzanian name meaning "joy."

The children stopped playing. They looked at me, wondering who these strangers were. I smiled and waved at them. The children edged their way closer to Kyesi.

We shook hands. I put my left hand on top of my right forearm as a sign of respect.

"It is good to meet you, Kyesi. We come from Kenya, from a home called Mully Children's Family. As you can see, we are in a group. Would it be all right if we joined you?"

She nodded. There were not enough chairs for all of us. I chose to stand. "These are my grandchildren," she said.

"I am Hannah. I am very happy to meet you," I said. I took a chance and reached out my hand. One of the boys eyed me, then reached out and shook my hand. The other boy did the same, but the girl remained shy at Kyesi's side. I waved at her.

"Thank you," I said to Kyesi. "It is very kind of you to let us speak with you."

She studied me, as if all her years of experience were filtering me through her many layers to determine if I was genuine or not.

"You have a kind heart," she said.

That caught me off guard. I did not know what to say. Not with everyone standing around me. "Thank you," I replied. The tone of her voice indicated to me that she was the kind of person I would enjoy knowing. "As do you."

Despite the large age gap between us, it felt like we could have been long-time friends.

"Can you tell me what brings you to me today?"

Time to say it. Time to be courageous. We had been turned down many times. The pastor had once gone to a bar to try to witness to people, and they had chased him out with a stick. People here in the slum had slammed doors in our faces. But the longer I was here, the more I realized that this was not about trying to get results as much as it was about being faithful. So I told her my reason as honestly as I could.

"I have come to tell you the Good News of Jesus Christ."

I was prepared for whatever response she would give. If she rejected me, that was fine. If she wanted to listen more, all the better. A sudden peace came over me. I felt the relief that came with knowing this was not about me. It seemed so natural. Like all I had to do was open the door, and the rest was up to God. I sensed the freedom that came with being consumed by a love for God and a love for this precious elderly woman.

"I see," she whispered. She glanced down the street as though to see if anyone was listening. She turned back to me. "I believe in many spirits," she said. "But they have not helped me." She leaned forward ever so slightly in her chair.

"I want to tell you that God loves you and that you are created by Him," I said. "I know we haven't known each other very long, but I wanted to ask you, Do you want to ask Jesus to forgive you, and do you want to believe in Him for eternal life?"

It was out there now. If there was any doubt about why I was there before, it was cleared away now. She remained quiet. I watched her eyes for any hint of what she might be thinking. It was a lot being presented all at once. Interesting how a critical decision about eternity can come down to a choice on a hot, sunny afternoon through an encounter with strangers. Her life hinged on her decision. Which should give anyone pause for concern.

"Can you help me understand what you mean?" she asked.

Her teeth were barely visible. Her voice quiet. In spite of all the commotion in the slum, we found ourselves in this quiet place.

"Sure," I said. I glanced back at the pastor as if to say *You can jump in any time now.* But he had the wisdom pastors have when they step back and allow people to trust Christ. He simply raised his eyebrows and nodded his head ever so slightly in a way we Africans understand as encouragement.

"Please," she said.

I could not get over how connected I felt with her. A few minutes before, I had never met her. How did this happen so quickly?

"I want to tell you that God made you and He loves you."

She blinked. It looked to me like the first slight onset of tears was beginning. Crying helps release emotions. But tears in a slum could really sting when the water mixed with all the dust in the air.

"You and I have sinned. This means we have done things like lying, cheating, thinking bad thoughts about others. And this separates us from God."

The nervousness left me. I did not need to think about being courageous anymore. I just spoke with her, the way friends do, and felt a deep love for her.

"We have no way to reach God. We can try to be good and do good things, but it won't be enough. It is like trying to swim across the ocean. He is just too far from us. It is impossible."

She pressed her lips together as a sign of conviction. She felt the accuracy of the description and the hopelessness that accompanied it.

"But there is hope," I continued. "God knew we could not make up for our sins. He wanted to give us His life. So He sent His Son Jesus to the earth. You and I are guilty of our sins. But Jesus took our place. He died on a cross. He took our sins, and He offers us life with Him forever."

She blinked again, squeezing out tears that ran down her cheeks.

"The Bible says 'For God so loved the world, that He gave His only begotten Son, that whoever believes in Him shall not perish, but have eternal life.' Would you like this life?" I asked.

She exhaled. Her shoulders dropped in relief, much the way a hiker relaxes after dropping a heavy pack from his back.

"Yes," she said.

Her reply came so quickly that it left me breathless. I wasn't sure what to expect but had assumed it would take longer to convince her.

"All right," I said. "Let's pray."

Without being asked to, and without me expecting that she should, she instinctively got off her chair to kneel down. She struggled to grab the back of the chair to steady herself. I stretched out my hand to help her, but by the time I reached her she already had her knees on the hard-packed ground. The children gathered around her, trying to understand what was happening. She folded her hands on the chair. She waited in holy silence. Then she whispered, "I don't know what to say."

"No problem," I said, kneeling down beside her. "You can repeat after me if you like." She nodded and did. "Dear God. Thank You for creating me. Thank You for loving me. Thank You for dying on the cross for my sins, Jesus. I ask You to forgive my sins. I turn away from my own life and give myself totally to You. I put my faith in You, and in You alone. I thank You that You have now made me Your child. Help me to follow You. Amen."

That was it. No big commotion, No celebration. Not down here on earth, anyway. She opened her eyes. Her tears were clear this time. They had managed to wash out all the dirt.

She looked at me with a different expression this time. No fear. No worry. If I felt I knew her before, I really felt I knew her now. We were sisters.

"Thank you," she said.

"You are most welcome, Kyesi."

"You have a special gift," she said. "You make people feel at ease. You don't judge them. You care deeply for people."

We heard the music again. As the others encouraged her I stayed focused on Kyesi's last words to me. What she said reached into me, spoke to me.

I turned to the others. The fun beat of the music caused them to sway to the rhythm. Her grandchildren began to play.

"Thank you," she said, looking to her grandchildren. "I have some work to do with these ones. To pass on what I have received."

"You are most welcome," I said. "Thank you for listening."

We hugged her and her grandchildren. I smiled to her as we walked back under the fast-sinking sun. Her face reflected the golden light. It was a moment I could stay in forever.

As the group discussed what we had just experienced, I too felt a burden slipping off my shoulders. Like my own heavy pack was falling off. But as I thought about it, I was not able to determine what the contents of my own pack were. It caused me to stop. I turned around again to look at Kyesi in the far distance, as if doing so could somehow help me make sense of what I was feeling. Kyesi walked into her hut with her grandchildren, probably to prepare supper. The picture of her standing with that genuine smile on her face lived on in my memory.

We spent the rest of the two-week mission trip performing, handing out food, and going from door to door. The more I shared the gospel, the more comfortable I became. I saw it as an extension of my relationship with God. And even when people refused, I left the situation in God's hands.

On the trip back home, I thought often of Kyesi. Of her kind words to me. Of her putting her faith in Christ. I also thought about the weight that started to be lifted from my shoulders. It made me wonder if something more than a mission trip had been going on for me in Tanzania. I wondered if in some way my life was being changed, too.

• • •

Our bus returned to Kenya in the late afternoon. I saw the MCF Ndalani sign, and I felt the joy that comes with being home again. We stopped outside the devotional area. Mommy and Daddy gave us each a welcome home. Many students had gathered. I looked through the crowd of people. There in the back stood a young girl with a smile on her face. This time the smile was one of reassurance. Of contentment. Of joy that we were together again.

I walked up to Zemira.

"Welcome back," she said as we hugged.

"It is great to see you again. Have you been studying hard?"

"Very hard."

"And have you been good? Have you listened?"

We both laughed. "I have been very good. And you? How was it?"

"It was great. Really, really great."

"Is it like Kenya?"

"Much hotter."

Zemira's mouth dropped open. Her eyebrows raised in amazement. "Hotter?"

"Yes."

"Than Kenya?"

"Can you imagine?'

"I thought we were the hottest place in Africa."

"You see. When you are with me, you will learn things."

"Maybe someday I will know things to teach you."

We laughed again. "So tell me," I said.

"What?"

"What do you mean, 'what?' Have you forgotten?"

"Forgotten what?"

"You see? You have. I cannot even believe it. You."

Zemira giggled. "Of course I remember. You want to know where we are going for our walk."

"Ah! You remember!"

"You are not tired?"

"There is always nighttime to sleep. Let's go."

"All right," she replied. "Follow me."

"And," I asked. "Where are we going?"

"For a walk among the mango trees!"

"Perfect," I said. "But the mangos are still in season, so I am not sure if I will get enough time to talk. I might be too busy eating!"

Zemira and I laughed as we dropped off my bag in my dorm, and we walked out to the trees. We asked Mommy if we could each pick a mango.

She smiled and said yes. The sun shone. The air smelled clean and fresh. A welcome change for me. I put my arm around Zemira.

We headed off to the mango trees.

"So," Zemira said. "I want to hear about your trip."

"Well," I said. "Let me tell you."

We ate mangos, then spent the rest of the day exploring the new trees that had been planted and exploring the new adventures that had been planted in each of our lives. It felt good to hear her speak of the future with such optimism. I had not heard that from her before MCF. I shared about Tanzania. She asked questions about every detail. About the people. The way Mbagala looked. How I felt about my time with Kyesi. When bedtime came, we wished each other a good night. I watched as she walked to her dormitory. Her steps were light. Her walking, brisk with joy. The sound of her flip-flops against the ground faded until it disappeared. We were together as a family again.

All 500 of us.

CHAPTER
twenty-four

I was having such a hard time catching my breath, I thought I was going to faint.

"We are almost there!" Isabella said. She turned back to look at me and smiled. How anyone could smile while running was way beyond me.

We had nearly completed our run around the football field, like we did every morning. And Isabella beat me to the finish line, like she did every morning.

"Actually, I need to correct you, Isabella. I think it is *you* who is almost there."

She laughed so hard she fell down. I caught up to her and collapsed to the ground. I would have said something to her, but all I could do was gasp for breath.

I had to hand it to Isabella. She was an incredible athlete. She took karate and made it all the way to black belt. That fact alone made me glad to be on her good side.

I felt my breathing returning to normal.

"This is embarrassing," I said.

"Why?"

"I am Kenyan. We are famous in the whole world for running. And look at me—I can barely keep up."

Isabella laughed. "You will make Kenya famous for being a great doctor."

"That is good."

"Why?"

"Because being a doctor does not require running a marathon."

We laughed again and got up.

It was time for breakfast.

• • •

Saturdays at MCF give each child a chance to focus on things that are dear to their heart. Some go on hikes way up to Pride Rock up on Mully Mountain. Some swim for hours in the Thika River. Me, I studied the entire morning. I read and reviewed all the notes and assignments from the previous week and read ahead to next week. After lunch I had planned on going for a swim, but I was suddenly overcome with a strong desire to write a song.

I had never written one before. And, like sharing the gospel in Tanzania, it felt like a daunting task to undertake. Wasn't I better off just singing other people's songs? That would have been fine. But I had learned the secret of listening when God speaks to my heart.

I went to my upper bunk and pulled out my pen and my special notebook. In this notebook I had written many of the songs we sang in choir. We did not have photocopiers, and so we needed to write out the words to each of our songs. We only had one master songbook. At MCF, you learned to memorize.

I turned to a blank page. Here I was. For the first time. Trying to compose a song.

My heart was filled with the desire to communicate. To share what was on my mind. But I found I had no idea what to write. I closed my eyes, dropped my head onto my pillow, and prayed.

Dear God. I really love to sing. I love to sing about You. And I want to write a song for You. But I do not know what I should compose. Please give me a song. I give this song to You to do whatever You like.

I waited.

Then I waited some more.

Then I stared at the blank page.

I resisted the urge to just write something for writing's sake. I suppose I could have put words down on paper. Just write anything down with the hope it would be good. But if it did not come from my heart—if it did not flow from God through my heart—then writing it down felt dishonest to me.

I wanted my song to be genuine. To be truthful. To be from God.

So I waited longer.

What's on your heart, Hannah?

I felt immediately at peace. I sometimes wondered if that's why I loved giraffes so much. They are such peaceful animals. That quality always attracted me to them. I quieted my thoughts. I relaxed my need to find something to say and concentrated instead on receiving something.

You have read so many passages in the Psalms. How would you describe them?

They are honest worship.

Exactly. What have I placed in your heart?

I searched my thoughts and my feelings.

I have this deep longing, Lord. A desire ...

And what do you desire?

I want to be with You. I want ... I want to praise You. I want to live with You forever, Lord.

The words began to pour through me. They came so fast I could barely write them down quickly enough.

I felt I had the start of a verse. But I needed to end it off ...

No matter. It would come later.

I closed my eyes. For a room that was filled with girls at night, it was surprisingly empty during the day. That was strange. Especially for a Saturday.

Just be honest. Be honest with Me about what has happened in your life. What was the biggest moment in your life?

In my life I had faced many problems. I had sickness. I had experienced an ongoing struggle in my mind. I felt a war between giving up and trusting in God. But the biggest moment of my life was when I came to know Him there at MCF. Everything changed when I prayed He would save me from my sins.

I wrote my thoughts down as fast as they came to my mind. It frustrated me that my hand could not write faster to keep up with my thoughts.

Two verses down. One more to go.

And what do you want to do now with your life?

I want to become a doctor.

And what do you want for other people?

I want all my brothers and sisters and everyone else I come into contact with to know You.

And why? Why do you want them to come to know Me?

Because they were orphans, poor, or alone on the streets. They can come to know You and find a safe place in You. You can give them eternal life so they will have victory over all the things that are attacking them.

I put my pen down. The rough outline was done.

I sat up in bed. I read my notes. I felt the uncanny connection of seeing words on a page that came to me from God. Yet there they were. Just simple lyrics to a song. Interesting that something so simple can be so powerful.

I hurried out of bed.

• • •

My friend Rebekah and I sat across from each other at a table in the children's centre. We became friends singing together in choir. Rebekah was such a calm person. She had a great laugh, too. If you heard someone laughing from far away, it was probably Rebekah. She helped me rework and rework and rework the lines. We crossed lines out that we thought didn't belong, then changed our minds and put them back in, then crossed others out. Each time we made a revision, we felt we came closer to a completed song. Sometimes it felt like we were going in circles, like when you are trying to solve a math problem and keep getting the wrong answer. But we stuck with it. We refused to give up. And we arrived at words we were convinced were right. We hummed melodies back and forth to each other, trying different rhythms until we settled on one that felt natural.

When we thought that we had a final draft of meaningful lyrics, we called Isabella and some of our other friends. We gathered together in an empty classroom and stood in a circle in our sandals on the concrete floor. A gentle breeze came in through the windows. It felt so good to spend an afternoon this way.

"Thank you for coming," I said. "We want to try this song out. It's new. I know because we just wrote it today."

They laughed. I felt blessed to have my friends help sing this song. The culture of supporting one another at MCF benefited us all. There was something freeing and kind about giving of myself to help someone in their dreams and about willingly receiving the help of others in accomplishing my dreams. That one spark of encouragement could go a long, long way.

We needed each other.

This is what we sang.

Natamani kutemeba nawe   *I desire to walk with You.*
Natamani kufurahi nawe   *I desire to rejoice with You.*
Natamani kuishi nawe   *I desire to live with You.*
Ewe baba Jehova   *Oh! Jehovah my Lord!*

Nashida nyingi zimenisumbua *I have been through a lot of problems,*
Magonjwa hata na vita   *Diseases and even war.*
Ewe Baba na kuomba   *I pray oh! Lord*
Uje unirehemu   *Come and save me.*

Ewe ndungu dada yangu   *Oh! My brother and sisters*
Uje kwake Yesu leo   *Come to Jesus today.*
Yeye ndiye tegemeo   *He is Your refuge.*
Atakushindia   *He will give You victory.*

I already had the words memorized, so I concentrated on how it felt to sing the song. How it felt to have God's presence with us in the room. How it felt to have the kingdom of God among us.

"It is really great," Isabella said after we finished.

You can always tell when your best friends are being honest with you. There is encouragement, and there is flattery. Flattery does not help anyone. And so we make it a practice to be encouraging and truthful.

"Thank you."

"You need to ask Dickson."

I had a sudden moment of nervousness at the thought of approaching our choir leader with my song. "What?"

"Ask him to sing it in our choir."

And the whole group agreed.

• • •

I waited quietly at the door. Choir practice was about to begin. Dickson spoke with one of our classmates. Just as he finished, I quietly called out to him. "Dickson?"

"Ah, Hannah!"

Like all of Mulli's biological children, Dickson had a massive smile. And like the others, Dickson had the incredible ability to connect with me. They were always so willing to help me, to spend time with me, to encourage me.

To love me.

"Do you have time to talk?" I asked. "I know choir practice is starting—"

He laughed. Such a loud, resonating laugh. It filled the entire room. "Time? Of course, Hannah. We have lots of time. We are in Africa. We always have time, right?"

I laughed. I handed him the pages of my song. As much as the others liked it, this was the real test.

He read the lyrics. His face softened as he studied the words. When he had finished, he spoke softly.

"Where did you get these?"

"I wrote them together with Rebekah. I was—"

"We have to sing it. Today. Hannah, this is excellent."

"You think so?"

"I know so." His bright smile came back. "Ready?"

"All right."

Dickson clapped his hands. Everyone quieted down.

"Thank you, everyone, for coming. We have something special today. Very special. Today, for our first song, we are going to sing a song Hannah and Rebekah have composed. They are going to introduce it to us."

The choir cheered. This kind of support can seem like a small thing. But for me it meant so much. We were each other's siblings, but we were also each other's biggest fans. I desired my siblings' success far more than my own.

And they felt the same way about me.

I believe this kind of environment helps propel us to achieve the calling of God on our lives.

I felt the rhythm in my feet. In my shoulders. In my heart. I sang the first note, and the moment I did, my shyness disappeared. I finished, and the room erupted in clapping.

"Hannah and Rebekah, it is tremendous!" Dickson said. "Praise the Lord."

And everyone clapped in agreement.

"All right, can we try it?" Dickson asked.

The group joined in, and we sang it again. Even though they had only heard it the one time, they began singing as if they had known the melody their whole lives.

Good songs often feel that way.

Daddy Mulli once told us that we are each created in a unique way. No two of us are the same. All people have unique fingerprints. All giraffes have a unique spot pattern. No two giraffes are created the same. Each of us has been individually created with certain gifts. And we need to develop those gifts. When we do, we fulfill what God designed us to be. I closed my eyes. As I sang the song God gave me, I sensed that I was doing what I was created to do. I sensed His presence. I sensed His goodness.

I glanced at Rebekah, who raised her eyebrows at me. We had spent the entire afternoon composing this one song.

And I had a feeling we had created something that would be sung for many years to come.

CHAPTER
twenty-four

O ur daddy loved the word *focus*. Whenever he talked to us about our relationship with God, our studies in school, our choir, sports, or other programs, he reminded us that we are to "be focused"—to be dedicated and of a single mind in pursuing what we are doing.

Our form 4 (grade 12) national exam was no exception.

The national exam covered everything we had learned. Not just in the current year, mind you. They covered everything in the subject all the way back to when we first started learning it. So you had to remember what you studied not only in form 4 but the previous years as well. This takes a lot of hard work and many hours of focused concentration.

We would be required to write an average of two exams per day. Nearly all of our subjects would have two exams each. On top of that, we had papers to write. The exam period would last a month. And it is a month no one forgets.

Our mandatory subjects included math, English, and Swahili. Our sciences required us to have taken either two or all three of chemistry, biology, and physics. I had all three. In addition, we had two to three humanities, like history, Christian Religious Education, and geography, from which I had studied CRE and geography. The last category was technical subjects, from which I had chosen to study music.

Each subject is awarded a grade, but our exams do not get marked by our own teachers. All exams are sent under seal to the government of Kenya to be marked. An average of the results of every person's subjects is taken to give one final overall grade. And that final grade is compared with every other form 4 student in all of Kenya. All of us knew that only the best got to go further.

And none knew it better than prospective medical students. A-plus was the goal. An A would be all right. Anything lower, and you would really be taking a chance. This knowledge had helped to motivate me during my studies. Nothing less than my absolute best and full concentration would do.

Receiving an invitation to university wasn't the only thing you needed. You also had to have money. No money, no university. On top of this, we were all in competition with other form 4 students across Kenya for such a few university spots.

I remembered the story Isabella told me about how our daddy was met with so much resistance when he tried to get MCF registered as an official school. *Street children and orphans will be a total failure,* the officials had said. But they were wrong. The government's highest authority overruled them and accredited us as a school. MCF students took the national exams, and we consistently achieved the highest grades.

With God, all things are possible.

This is what I kept saying to myself as I studied each day late into the evening. Night after night, the students crammed together into classrooms, studying for many hours. Normally during our evening study you would hear some joking around. At least a couple of people would be talking to each other. But not in the weeks and days leading up to exams. You felt a thick fog of tension in the air. We all knew what was riding on our performance in the next month. No one needed to remind us.

In some respects, having lived through difficult beginnings gave us a resilient perspective on life. I sometimes think the reason people worry is because deep down inside they wonder if they will be able to handle it if they end up at the bottom of the world. For those of us who had been there, for those of us who had the soles of our feet on the very bottom of what this world has to offer, we had confidence knowing that if Christ could bring us up out of that, we could trust Him with anything else that came our way.

We studied and crammed like millions of other students in every country around the world. I had gone over and over everything. I reached the point where I thought I could close my eyes and see the pages in my mind. I was ready. Tomorrow would be my first exam.

I walked back to the dormitory with Isabella. Normally I would have looked up at the stars and admired them. But the pressure of the studies had exhausted me, and I just wanted to get to bed.

"We have been studying so long," Isabella said.

"It has been a lot of work."

Gone was the memory of us laughing on the football field after we went running. I heard the concern in her tone of voice. She, I am sure, heard it in mine as well. It all came down to this.

"I am praying for you, Isabella."

"Thank you. And I am praying for you, too," she said. I loved the sound of her voice. A deep, resonating honesty that reflected her character. "Hannah?" Isabella whispered.

"Yes."

"I'm worried," she said.

"It is a lot to have on our minds. What in particular are you worried about?"

"The not-knowing," she said. "I do not know what tomorrow will bring."

"I agree. From now on, they should give all students the test questions a full week before."

Isabella laughed. "That would help."

It broke the tension for a moment, allowing us the brief chance to escape before returning to reality.

"We try to prepare as much as we can. But we don't really know for sure what is coming, so we wonder if we are as prepared as we need to be," I said.

I felt her exhale. She turned to me, and we shared a glance. I understood. And she felt that I understood.

"That's exactly it," she said.

"Isabella, you have really done your best. God understands. You have done your part. Now you need to trust Him and leave it in His hands."

"Thank you, Hannah. You always know just what to say to make me feel better. I wish I could do the same."

"You do, Isabella."

"Promise?"

"Promise."

Reaching the dormitory, we gave each other a hug. During exam time, I slept in my old dorm with Isabella, giving me a chance to focus on my studies. We opened the door quietly, got into our beds, and closed our eyes. Both of us hoped for a good night's rest.

We were going to need it.

• • •

We sat down in the same seats. The same concrete floor beneath us. The same wood trusses above. The same classmates in their same places. The classroom looked the same.

But it felt different.

This was it. My studies were all these years in the making. Strange to think it all came down to this gruelling month. The teacher gave instructions not to begin until he said so. He placed exam papers on our desks, face down. I stared at the back of the page. I felt my pulse begin to quicken. No matter how much you prepare yourself, you can't quite prepare for the moment when it comes right down to it. I prayed. Took in a breath.

"Begin."

I heard the swoosh of papers being turned over. I read the first question.

I knew the answer.

• • •

The exam period proved to be more exhausting than any of us could have imagined. After finishing each exam, we shoved the previous topic out of our minds and switched gears to focus solely on the next subject. The intense concentration took its toll. One evening during preps I found myself staring at the chalkboard and could not immediately remember if it was morning or evening. Or if I was awake or dreaming.

The last exam finally came and went. Oh, that feeling of stepping outside the classroom and having the sun melt away my stress! MCF turned back to the way I remembered it. I noticed the bright red flowers for the first time since exams started. It was like I had escaped from that fog.

"We're done!" I said to Isabella as she emerged from the room.

Her eyes were glazed over. She thought for a moment. Looked at me with a quizzical expression.

"Do we have time for a run?" she asked.

We laughed. We could do anything now.

We had all the time in the world.

• • •

It was a full month before the exam results came in. Somebody once said the waiting is the hardest part. I would have to agree. Word spread through MCF that we could check our results that afternoon. We all felt that nervous tug in our hearts.

We had to line up outside the education office. The way it worked is we were allowed to go into the office one at a time. The teacher would show us the list of names and point to our grade. One by one, students went in, and one by one they came out. Some were thrilled. Some were content. Some were devastated. Those of us in the lineup could only wait our turn.

I felt the tension in my arms. My pulse quickened. Strange that, next to being accepted at MCF, finding out our national exam results was one of the most important announcements we would receive.

God help me. God help me.

Then it was my turn.

My sandals clicked against the floor. I stepped through the open brown door. The head of education looked up from behind his desk at the back of the room. He acknowledged me, giving no hint at my results, then looked down at the list of names. He turned the paper in my direction and put his finger beside my name. I stepped closer.

I lowered my eyes, following down to his finger. I saw my name. I began glancing to the right. I felt excitement building in my heart. All these long years. All these hours of hard work. My gaze made it across the line.

I saw my mark.

I felt the blood rush out of my face. My eyes stayed locked on the grade. I felt my pulse throb in my throat. Then I felt it in my ears. It was so loud, it would have been easier to have had someone screaming at me at the top of their lungs.

At first I thought I had read wrong. My mind had already decided what the result was going to be before I walked in. But fact has a way of disrupting dreams with cold, hard reality. I continued staring, but as much as I wished, it did not change the result.

I had not made it.

I hadn't even come close.

In a futile last attempt, I looked back at my name and read across in the unlikely chance I had made a mistake and misread the grade.

No such fortune.

"You have really tried hard," he said.

I didn't care. His words didn't matter. That I had tried hard only made it worse. Had I slacked off and gotten this useless grade I would have at least had the solace of believing that I could have gotten the grade I needed had I worked hard.

But I had worked hard.

I had prayed.

And I hadn't made it.

I felt my throat close. Without meaning to, I held my breath. If the teacher said something more, I did not hear it. I blinked, hoping maybe this was a dream and I could wake up from it to a better result.

But it wasn't a dream. And with that went my last chance to erase what happened and to try to start over again. To create a different result for myself.

But the mark was in. I was out of time. And there was nothing left for me to do to change my situation.

I said nothing. What could I possibly? My body was in total shock. It felt like someone had hooked me up to an electrical current. I wasn't able to move for what seemed like hours. What got me motivated to leave was not wanting to see that grade anymore. I did not want my eyes to register that image any longer. I breathed again. But the life had totally left my body. I felt like collapsing to the floor.

I turned and walked out, wishing I could disappear.

As I left the office, others tried to talk to me. I could not respond to them. I ran back to the dormitory, already regretting all the years of effort I had put into my schooling. Many of my classmates saw me. I tried to hold back my tears, but I had as much success as a sailor does who tries to hold back the waves. I felt the unbearable anguish of failure, defeat, and despair crashing over me.

I wanted to become a doctor. I loved helping people. I loved serving in the medical camps. It gave me so much joy to see a person get better. Wasn't that a sign? Wasn't that confirmation? Hadn't we prayed and prayed and prayed about this?

I pulled open the blue door to the dormitory. It was empty. And as much as I needed someone right then, I was just as glad to have a place where I could be alone.

I lay face down in my bed, sobbing into my pillow. What had just happened? What in the world had just gone so wrong? I felt the tears soaking my pillowcase. I lifted my head. I saw my blue-and-white Bible stuck in between the frame and the mattress. How many hours had I read it?

You left me, God. You walked out on me when I needed You most. I trusted You. And You abandoned me. You let me down when I needed You the most.

I understood better now what the disciples felt like in that boat during the storm when Jesus was sleeping.

I did not know what to think. I did not know how to stop feeling so awful. All I could see was that horrible grade that had now been burned into my mind. And try as I might, I could not switch the scene. I hadn't just missed my goal; I had completely blown it.

I felt embarrassed for having believed I could become a doctor.

I felt terrible for letting Daddy and Mommy down.

I did not even have the courage to hold my Bible. I found it difficult to pray. I felt consumed with loss again. It felt like everything I had worked towards—everything I had given myself for all those years—was now a complete and total waste of time. Everything in my life had fallen apart.

Again.

What was the point of me even being at MCF if I was going to fail like that? I shouldn't have been here. I shouldn't have been picked. I had taken the spot of someone else who could have made better use of this incredible opportunity.

And all of this left me wondering what in the world could possibly happen next.

CHAPTER
twenty-six

It came as no relief to me when a student entered the room to tell me that Daddy Mulli wanted to meet with the entire form 4 class in 15 minutes. It was like having a meeting with the runners of a race and you were the one who came in last. I wanted to escape. I wanted to disappear. I wanted to keep my head buried in my pillow.

Forever.

But we never wanted to disobey our daddy, and so I tried to force my feet onto the floor. My body lay there in limbo—half of me on my bed, the other half off. I struggled to understand what I worried about more—facing my Daddy and the other children and admitting to them that I failed, or admitting my failure to myself.

I pushed the rest of my body and sat up in bed. My face staring down at the concrete floor at nothing in particular. I heard a knock at the door. I did not answer. I did not want to. The door opened. I heard feet quietly stepping into the room and stopping at the door.

Who was it? Isabella? Mommy? Daddy? I waited. The other person waited. Finally, I looked up.

Zemira stood looking at me with all the wisdom that caring people have when they realize words are not nearly as needed as a person's presence is. I don't know why, but seeing her made me cry again. It was as if being with the person I had known the longest gave me a sense of how long this journey had really been.

She had been with me from the start. From when I had the desire to become a doctor, to studying at MCF. To this. She sat down next me, saying nothing but speaking volumes. I leaned into her, and she into me. I was out of words. The shock of disbelief still overwhelming me. Sitting next to Zemira helped me remember that person I was so long ago before the dream of medicine started. Strange to think there was a time when I did not know I wanted to be a doctor. It had consumed me. Driven me. Filled my thoughts and dreams for years. And now, it seemed to have come full circle. I was back to the time when it was just Zemira and me and no medicine.

I did not know who I was without my dream.

It had all been taken from me.

Yet here I was. And having Zemira beside me helped me realize that there was a Hannah who existed prior to all of this.

The same student returned to the door.

"Daddy Mulli is ready now for the form fours," he whispered, seeing my pain. I nodded. He nodded as well. We had all been there at one time or another.

Zemira gave me a hug. She got up and walked to the door. She glanced back. I looked up to her. We made eye contact. She walked out. I heard her footsteps as she left.

Sometimes the younger help the older.

I stood to my feet. The door looked so far way. I walked for what seemed like much longer than it usually took to reach it. I turned the handle. The bright sunshine illuminated me. Normally this would have brought a smile to my face. Today it only further served to remind me that there was no place to hide.

Opening the blue door, I slipped on my sandals and began what felt like a marathon distance walk. I took the path behind the kitchen towards Thika River. There would be fewer people on this route. Fewer people I would have to encounter. Fewer people with whom I would have to make eye contact. But my detour was pointless, really. With so many children on the property, I was bound to be seen.

I had learned about the dangers of hiding my feelings, but it was still hard to fight that instinct.

As I walked past the trees where Mommy Esther and I talked all those months before, I remembered the words she said. *You are beautiful because God has made you. Always remember that.*

I wished He would have also made me smarter.

Hearing people walking nearby, I quickened my pace as they headed off in another direction. I would later feel bad for not looking up to at least try to smile at them. In the distance, I saw the umbrella thorn tree. It did not hold the same majestic look it once had. I used to admire it, be enthralled by it. Now, it just looked average. Taking the dirt trail, I headed down to the flat area on the bank of the Thika River. I recalled the meeting Mommy Esther had with all of us girls as we sat down on the benches. She taught us about being women of God.

You can see the trees around you. They draw their strength from the water through their roots. In the same way, we trust God to give us His strength into our lives to accomplish His purpose.

Her talk made sense to me then. It made no sense now.

To the far left, I saw Daddy Mulli's outdoor office. Ahead of me I saw the benches where my classmates had gathered. In the distance, I saw the Thika River and heard the water rushing past. *Water follows its course.*

I saw four of the boys sitting on one of the benches, joking and laughing. Two of them were very smart. I am sure they had both received an A or even an A-plus. The other two were not quite as good at school. Yet all four of them were laughing so hard, bugging each other. One of them actually fell off the bench, he was howling so hard.

It was like they understood that there was a life outside of their grades. And I admired them for it.

I sat down at an empty spot by myself. Isabella noticed and left her seat to sit beside me.

"Ooo-aye," Daddy Mulli said from the front.

The others responded back with the same greeting. I did not. I remembered the first time I heard that expression. Daddy Mulli gave it at the devotion time when I first arrived at MCF with Uncle Raza and my sister, Zemira. At the time, I had not even realized that the man speaking at the front was Daddy Mulli. I found it unfortunate that a group setting back then was so full of hope and new adventures, and sitting here now with many of those same classmates, it marked nothing more for me than faded dreams.

"You have all worked very hard," Daddy Mulli said. "And now we have the results. Some of the results for you have been exactly what you hoped for. And some of you even received higher grades than you thought you would."

Daddy raised his hand to chest height. "You thought that you were going to be here." Then he raised it above his head. "And you got all the way up here."

Some students laughed. I wished I could have.

"For some of you, this is a great day. You are going to university. Can you imagine? Look where God has brought you from. All the way from the streets; from the slums; from many, many hard situations. But God rescued you. He brought you here, to Mully Children's Family. And now you are going to go to even higher places."

I knew some of my classmates also wanted to become doctors. With the results they received, some of them would be on their way. In my heart, I knew I felt happy for them. In some way, it was a good distraction from my own situation. At least for the time being.

"But there are times when what we hope for does not happen. Our hearts can be dashed. We work and we work and we work. We work so hard. And then we come to the end, and it seems like our hard work did not pay off. It did not happen. It is such a shock. And in our hearts, we feel so bad. So bad. Even me, I remember. I was in school, and I did my very best. And I worked digging holes as best as I could. But I could not get the money for tuition, and I had to leave school. It was all over. This is what I thought. I had nothing that I could do but go back into a field and continue digging."

I felt my eyes begin to well up with tears. I did not immediately understand why. I had experienced this many times before with Mommy and Daddy. When someone understands, when they can reach you with what you are feeling, you feel your heart beginning to heal.

And sometimes that healing starts with crying.

"I dug holes every day. In the hot sun. You all know what it is like here in Kenya. So hot. And there I had to dig. And this is what I thought my life would be. All my dreams, all my hopes, everything that I wanted in life. Gone. Vanished. Totally disappeared with no chance of getting them back. I had done everything. Absolutely. And now, I was at the very bottom. The total end of everything. This is what I thought."

I could relate.

"It was like Jonah. Who remembers the story of Jonah?"

The students nodded.

"He was thrown off the ship. He landed in the water. And he was sinking. 'Surely,' he thought, 'this is now the end.' But then, God reached out to him with the big fish. And even me, God reached out to me. He saved me. And slowly He changed my life. Why am I telling you this?"

I felt a calmness come over me. Relief, if even temporary, for the battle raging in my mind.

"In life, what we see as the ending, God sees as a beginning. What we see as hopeless, our Father in heaven sees as hope for a new start. Many of you had no father. But God brought you in. And spiritually—the most important—we were all orphans before we met Jesus Christ. He forgave our sins, and we put our faith in Him. That is when God turned everything around, and He became the Father to the fatherless."

He paused. He could have talked for hours. And much of me wished that he would have.

"And so, if you have done a great job and received a high mark, we all celebrate with you. And if you have not achieved what you desired, remember, God has a plan for you."

In my mind, I agreed with what he was saying. But in my heart it felt like his words applied to everyone else except me.

"I want all of you, one by one, to say your grade for us to hear."

I wanted to turn invisible and crawl under the wooden bench. I wanted to wake up from this dream.

"When we say it out loud, it makes it real. If we did great, we rejoice. If we did not reach our goal, we need to be clear in our minds that it has happened. We need to face reality. We cannot live in shame or in fear of our disappointments. Fear can have great control over us if we keep things hidden. Saying our score brings it out into the open. And remember, we are all family here, and so we support one another."

Daddy Mulli looked to one of the boys sitting at the far back whom I had seen earlier.

"A-plus," the boy said. I heard the gasps in amazement.

"B," the next person said.

I found it hard to hear each of them say their scores out loud. A, B, and C were all passing grades. But we all knew that to do well in university you needed the higher marks.

It would soon be my turn to state my grade.

"B-plus," the girl at the end of the row said. "C," said the next. "B," the boy beside me said.

Then came the moment when it was my turn. Only a second or two had passed since the last person spoke, but to me it felt like an eternity. I felt my blood pressure rise. It was as if the whole world had suddenly stopped and everyone was looking at me.

I tried to be courageous. There was no easy way to do this. And so with fear and embarrassment I spoke out.

"D-plus."

No one said anything. They didn't have to. The quiet said it all. They felt bad for me. I tried not to think of that. Having people feel sorry for me always made me want to cry. And even though there were still more tears available, I really did not want to break down here. No thank you.

Isabella was next. B was a super grade. I knew in the tone of her voice. Friends know exactly the slightest variation in tone. And even though it was just one letter, the way she said it made me know that she was happy with it. Good for her.

The rest of the group gave their marks. I did not hear them. It's hard to hear anything when you feel like a total failure. When we had all finished, Daddy Mulli spoke.

"For those of you who have received a mark that will enable you to go to university, I will do my very best to get the money for you to go. Even if there is no money, we will pray for God to provide money. Just like the woman—the widow at Zarephath—who had no food. Elijah prayed, and God provided flour and oil for the woman. In the same way, I want to pray for Almighty God to provide you with funds to enable you to go to university. Can we stand?"

We stood. My legs felt as heavy as rock. I pushed my disappointment aside and in my heart prayed for my siblings to be given the money to attend university.

"Our loving God. You are our provider. You have given us food, clothing, shelter, and You have given us Your precious Son, who has given us eternal life. Lord, You said 'Ask, and it will be given to you; seek, and you will find; knock, and it will be opened to you.' And so, as our Father, we are asking You to provide for us now again. Many years ago, You enabled us to become an accredited school when many said they would not allow it. But You made it possible. A real miracle. And now, we ask You, O Jehovah God, to intervene and to bless Your children with money to go to university. We ask that You open the ways for blessings to come so that their dreams can be accomplished and that they will use their gifts to serve You. We thank You in Jesus' name. Amen."

I did my best not to cry, but the tears poured down my cheeks anyway. Daddy dismissed the students. One by one they left. Isabella waited for me, but Daddy asked only me to stay behind. Isabella said goodbye and walked up the hill, glancing back at me over her shoulder with a concerned expression.

Daddy and Mommy walked towards me. Mommy sat down beside me. Daddy sat down across from me. I wiped my tears as best I could. I am not sure why.

"I know this is not easy for you," Mommy said. "But we want to tell you that we love you very much."

I nodded. I knew this. But it was good to hear it anyway.

"Hannah," Daddy said. "Despite the mark you have received, you should not give up. I am here to help you in this situation, and in whatever situations you pass through. I want to encourage you to trust God. This is not the end of everything."

That was good to hear. Because it sure felt like it was the end.

"When things look their worst, God is still planning," Mommy said. "He is still working. Still leading. He works high above our understanding. And sometimes that means we cannot understand what He is doing. Or even why He is doing it."

Daddy nodded his head in agreement.

"What your mother has said is correct. I agree. We do not know the mind of God. And so, I want to tell you that I will make sure that you receive higher education in something else. Due to the grade, you will not get into medicine. You have acknowledged this with what you said. Now you need to decide on something different. You need to pray and choose a different course to take."

Even though I had hoped for a different direction, even though I had wanted, and still wanted, to go into medicine, I found his words to be both practical and wise.

"Remember," Daddy said. "Faith is believing God is in control, even when everything seems out of control."

"Thank you," I said.

"Come, let's go help with making dinner," Mommy said.

I didn't want to go. I wanted to stay by myself and wallow in my disappointment. She knew this, of course. She knew it would not be good for me to be by myself. So she stood and waited, with the love mothers have when they don't take no for an answer. I stood as well. She laughed and put her arm around me, and the three of us walked up the hill together.

In my mind, I knew this marked the end of medicine for me. It was gone. Gone for good. Still my heart clung to it. I found it difficult to really let it go. Strange that my mind understood what my heart failed to grasp. Why was that exactly?

It was time for a new pursuit. Time for a new passion. Time for a complete change of direction.

And I had no idea what that direction would be.

CHAPTER
twenty-seven

S ometimes you make the most progress by not moving anywhere.
 I did not have a clear sense of anything I should be pursuing. I had thought about going in a great many directions, but to me they did not feel like convictions. They felt like fleeting desires to chase for the sake of feeling that I was making progress. But ten steps in the wrong direction are not as fruitful as one step in the right direction. So, the following year was a time of waiting. Of listening. Of learning. I felt like a traveller at a train station with my bags packed, ready to go, yet unsure of which train to board. Or whether to board any train at all.

Without any clear confirmation about which direction to take, I decided it best to stay at MCF. Daddy accepted my request to be a volunteer in the hospitality department. I loved to help people and to make them feel welcome. This gave me a chance to serve other people and to spend time in prayer, seeking God.

Sometimes it helps to forget yourself.

I served guests who came to MCF from all over the world. Medical mission teams. Visitors. Volunteers. They came with incredible hearts for the children, the community, and the Lord. I saw how God brought people from everywhere to help in our humble home in Kenya.

I prayed a lot that year. I also spent a lot of time reading my Bible. I sought God more earnestly that year than any of my previous years.

And yet I heard the least from Him.

It's been said that God's silence is a gift to us. That seemed odd to me at first. I would have preferred for God to speak to me. To have Him say anything.

And perhaps He was speaking without me even knowing it.

A familiar story in the Gospels caught my attention. One evening, I read of the disciples in a boat during a storm. They were in complete distress. Jesus was sleeping. They woke Him and told Him how scared they were and even went so far as to inquire if He cared that they were going to drown. Jesus asked them why they had such little faith. And then He calmed the storm.

I used to think this passage meant that all I needed to do was pray hard so that God would calm the storms in my life. But this time I saw something more. Something deeper. Jesus always taught something about Himself to His disciples. But they did not understand the point of the lesson. Jesus had fallen asleep, but the three-in-one God was still in complete control, even when the storm seemed to be totally out of control. He calmed the storm not to show His disciples that they had to convince Him of their problems but to show them that He knew of their problem all along and was in complete control despite the storm. And if He was in complete control of the disciples' lives in the midst of a terrible storm, then I should be encouraged that He was also in control of my situation.

God was silent.

But He was not absent.

The more I prayed, the more I read the Bible, the more I felt in my heart that I needed to give everything into God's hand. This sounded simple enough. But I knew from my daddy's life that it took time to follow a calling. To be obedient. To let go.

Daddy heard God speaking to him, telling him to give up all his money and all his businesses. He heard God tell him to dedicate his life to helping rescue street children, orphans, and other destitute children.

But it took three years until he finally came to the end of himself and to give himself fully to God. That's when everything changed for him. I wanted that kind of change in my life.

I sensed God speaking to me as well. *Let go*, is what I continually heard Him say. At first I told God that I *had* let everything go. I had failed at getting into medicine, and I had accepted that. Wasn't that good enough? Wasn't that letting go?

And it took months for me to realize that, in fact, no, that was not letting go. Being denied access to medical school was not the same as me giving it up. I knew, logically, that the dream of becoming a doctor was over. But in my heart I still wanted it.

And I did not know how to reconcile those two differences.

One evening I stayed awake late in my bed, long after the lights had been turned out. My thoughts turned over in my mind, and I felt the frustration that comes with trying to force them out, only to have them gain more strength and keep me from sleeping. I sat up and pushed my back against the frame. I folded my hands and rested them and my forehead onto my lifted knees. The moonlight cast a glow into our room. I saw it reflect on my Bible lying beside me. I closed my eyes.

I told myself, *Being a doctor has become a huge part of your life. I know that it is wrong to continue to want this.*

Why do you still want it?

Why did I still want medicine even though I knew there was no chance for me to go to university to study it? It was like my brain was feeding my heart information, but my heart had put up a wall, saying, *No, I will not accept that.*

And that's when I realized where that wall came from.

I had built it myself.

I took a good thing of becoming a doctor, and I made it into the most important thing. I feel ashamed of this, but I wanted to become a doctor more than anything else. I am hanging on to it so dearly. Please, God, help me to let go of it once and for all. I can't fix myself. I just give everything to You.

And in that moment, I was free. That weight I felt begin to slip off my shoulders in the slum in Tanzania—it fell off altogether. I no longer felt shame over not having achieved my goal. I no longer felt a tension between fact and feeling. The need to be a doctor was truly gone. I could breathe again.

Thank You, God. Thank You for clearing my heart.

Then I began to hear God speak to me in a way other than silence. I heard Him in my heart. In my spirit.

The time you were with Mommy at the mango tree. She taught you that you are beautiful. Then she told you about a gift that you have. What did she say?

I thought back to the lesson of the ripe and the unripe mangos. About not judging someone by their outside appearance. And then she stopped. She looked at me with deep affection. With deep understanding.

What did she say to me?

I tried to recall. I could see her standing there and remembered her expression. She became so quiet. Then I remembered she said, *You have a gift of being able to connect with people. I see you when you talk to Isabella and to the little children. They are comfortable around you. They feel safe that they can share their heart.*

I did not realize it at the time, but she was telling me something important, perhaps without her even knowing it.

But what did she mean by that? And why was it important now?

Now think back to the time with Kyesi in Tanzania. What did she say to you?

I recalled the mission trip we made to Dar es Salaam. I remembered the elderly woman sitting on a chair in the slum. I remembered how she gave her life to Christ. What did she say to me?

After she got up from kneeling in the slum she said to me, *You have a special gift. You make people feel at ease. You don't judge them. You care deeply for people.*

Her words had impacted me then, and recalling them now they impacted me just as much.

But why? What was it about her words that encouraged me so much?

I tried to understand what these two sayings spoken by two different people meant. I sensed that there was an answer within them, but my mind could not assemble the pieces.

And Isabella. What did she tell you when you were walking with her after studying for exams? She was so concerned. She confided in you. What did she say?

I remembered that evening well. We studied so long that night. She was worried about her exams. We both were. I encouraged her on our walk back to the dormitory. *You always know just what to say to make me feel better.*

It was all there right in front of me. Why could I not put this together? Why could I not see the obvious answer? All of them saying the same thing, essentially. That God had used me to encourage them. To help them. To listen to them.

What would the final picture look like when I assembled all these pieces?

At the medical mission you served people. After the medical examinations were completed, what did you do?

I did not understand. I volunteered. I helped the doctors and nurses from morning to night. That's all I did. I—no, that was not all. What did I do after the medical examinations?

Daddy Mulli commented to you on what he saw you do. What did he tell you?

I recalled closing the door of the clinic after cleaning up after everyone had left. I met with Daddy. What did he tell me?

You have a wonderful, gentle spirit with a deep compassion for people. You have this. You do. Nobody told you that you had to talk to the people after they received their medical help. But you did. From your heart. You went and talked and listened to people share about their problems. Many people have no one to talk to. But you made yourself available.

I thought back to the times when I spoke with the patients after they received their medication. I loved to listen to them. I loved hearing their stories, encouraging them, and praying with them. Many had mental, emotional, or relational problems in addition to their medical issues. Their minds and hearts needed healing as much as their bodies.

It was something that felt so natural for me to do. To meet with people and love them.

And down by Thika River. After the form 4 class had met. What did Daddy Mulli say to you?

I recalled the feeling of having to say my grade for everyone to hear. Yes, it was difficult. But it was also important. It was important to face reality. Afterwards, Daddy and Mommy spoke to me. What did he say at the very end? He had said earlier he would help me in another course. But then his very last line ... what did he say?

It came back to me.

Faith is believing God is in control, even when everything seems out of control.

I thought about what the others had seen in me. What they had said. Then I thought about my time growing up, before I came to MCF—when there was no one to help me out of my troubles. People had tried, but no one knew how to reach me. I had felt so confused, and there was no one to help me by explaining what was going on inside of me.

And that's when I realized it.

What if I could be used to reach people who were in trouble? What if I could be there to encourage and support them? I saw how others had confirmed this gift in me many times. But I was not able to see it because I was so focused on what I wanted to do.

I wanted to care for people. I had a heart for wanting people to be better. But I had assumed that this meant being a doctor and caring for their physical needs. Mommy said I was created in a beautiful way by God. For me this meant to look after not their physical ailments but the hurts of their hearts and their minds.

And in that moment, in the moonlight, on my bed, I finally had total peace.

• • •

The next morning, I hurried as fast as I could to find Daddy Mulli. I would like to say that I was running, but, as Isabella could confirm, what I do cannot be considered running by Kenyan standards. So I hurried. I hurried really fast.

After asking people where Daddy might be, I found him out in the French bean fields, examining the crops that would be exported to Europe to help pay for the expenses of the home. He finished speaking with one of the lead hands in the field. Daddy wore a yellow shirt, brown pants, and a brown leather hat that a friend had given to him. Some people joked that he should now be called Indiana Mulli.

He turned to see me. As usual, his eyes lit up with joy. As usual, his voice had the genuineness that came from his humble heart. And as usual, his smile made me feel welcomed and loved.

"Hello, Hannah! How are you this morning?"

"I am fine."

"Wonderful. And how did you sleep?"

"I slept well. Thank you."

"That is good. I am so glad to hear this."

"I wanted to come to talk to you."

"Wow! You came all this way to me out here in the field. That is a real honour for me, Hannah."

It was a gift he had. There was no other way to say it.

"Thank you. And I also want to say thank you for caring about me."

"Sure. Of course."

He became quiet. I felt the assurance that thousands of us felt when we came to speak to our dad.

"I have really thought about what you said to me. And for a long time I have been praying."

"Oh yes. I know. You have been praying for a long time. A very long time. Every day you are praying and reading your Bible and trusting the Lord."

"The Lord showed me the times when I had been used to touch people. Isabella. The woman in Dar es Salaam. The patients at the medical mission. And both you and Mommy have commented on this."

Daddy Mulli nodded in agreement. "And what have you decided?"

I felt no pressure. No anxiety. Just comfort and peace. Like a calm sea after a storm.

"There were many times when I was younger that I did not know what was going on with me. I needed help. And I received so much help here at MCF. And it is in my heart that I want to be able to help other people. I want to use my life story and how God has helped me to give hope to other people," I said.

Daddy looked into my eyes. I knew before I continued that he was going to support me.

"I would like to study to become a counsellor."

Daddy Mulli's smile confirmed what I had already received in my heart. I saw his agreement in the expression of contentment that came over him. I felt valued and ready for a challenge.

Girls need their dad's approval.

"I support you one hundred percent in this," he said. "And the Lord will help you to bring it to pass. You can count on Him through everything."

CHAPTER
twenty-eight

As I entered college that fall, I wondered what it would be like to study in a school other than MCF, to be in a place that was not home. Would I have friends? Would I be all right living in a different home?

Would I succeed?

Even though I had lived on MCF property most of my life, I found it surprisingly easy to fit into my new surroundings. The classes went well. I played volleyball with my new friends. We laughed a lot. I passed my tests. I sensed I was in the right place.

The late evenings I spent studying never felt like late evenings. Instead, they felt like a natural extension of the desires of my heart. This was no longer about me wanting to achieve something. It was about me wanting to serve people in the way God had designed for me. And this took the pressure off of performing for a result.

In my courses, I learned about the importance of prayer in counselling. If I thought I could use my own wit and compassion to help someone, then that person would not truly be helped. I learned that in every situation there is sin. And sin requires forgiveness. Forgiveness involves releasing someone who has wronged me, asking forgiveness of someone

I have wronged, or understanding that we live in a fallen world and we experience the pain that brings. By understanding the spiritual dimension of a problem, I was able to see the true need of a person. To see their problem in light of the cross.

This made intuitive sense to me because I had seen this type of counselling from Daddy and Mommy Mulli.

I also learned the importance of having good listening skills by being patient and loving with people in order to understand them. Good listeners resist giving people solutions to their problems. Instead, they offer a place to hear people, build trust, and bring the issues before God. People do not often have a place to share their heart. I felt this when I was young. There are times in life when, if you don't have God, you simply do not know where to turn or whom to approach. It's strange to think that, in a world of increasing population and increasing technology, we are more dissociated than ever. And I think this contributes to the problem—the idea that, given so many people around us and so many ways to communicate, it should be easy to connect with at least someone.

And yet it is easier than ever to be alone in a crowd.

I discovered that the critical moment comes when a person understands their need to look to Jesus. It is a mountain of an effort to lift our eyes up to Him. But this is good counselling. This is what the children of Israel had to do in the desert when they were bitten by the serpents. They had to look to the bronze serpent that Moses lifted up. And those who looked, lived. Jesus retells this story just before the most famous verse of all.

As Moses lifted up the serpent in the wilderness, even so must the Son of Man be lifted up; so that whoever believes will in Him have eternal life.

I was only made well with Jesus. I could not expect anyone else to be well without Him.

• • •

I completed my college program in counselling. The exams went well. That was an answer to prayer. Even though I did not know what would happen after graduation, I had the unmistakable feeling that my future was as solid as the concrete floor I felt under my feet whenever our choir sang at MCF.

Still, I wondered where God would have me serve next.

• • •

The Kibera slum was both the best and the most difficult place for me. The best because I loved to be with the people. And the most difficult because it broke my heart to see their lives.

Kibera means "forest" or "jungle." But this does not give an accurate impression of how the Kibera slum looks. There are hardly any trees in this slum, but it is still very much a jungle.

Kibera is one of the largest slums in Africa. Strictly speaking, Kibera is considered part of Nairobi. But the people feel as if they are in the middle of nowhere. Poverty cuts people off from the rest of civilization, and Kibera is no exception.

As was the case in the Mbagala slum we served at in Tanzania, people rarely own their own homes in Kibera. They rent. Their day consists of working long hours. By the end of the week, month, year, whichever, they are never further ahead than they were the one before. It is an endless cycle of poverty with little to no chance of escape.

The poor are dear to Daddy's heart. He visits the slums often. He approached me one evening after I babysat children for the day at MCF Yatta. "We are going on a mission to Kibera slum," he said. "I would like you to join us."

There was no other place I would have wanted to be. Daddy once said *we are born to serve*. And I understood why. When I let everything go, when I truly surrendered everything at the cross of Christ, my heart always became filled with the desire to serve those in need.

"I would be happy to be part of the team," I said. "Thank you for asking me."

• • •

We arrived in Kibera in our large Mully Children's Family bus. Kibera looked similar to other slums. Dilapidated rusty brown shacks made of metal and mud jammed together filled each side of the roads. The odd blue-painted door or bright red storefront provided the occasional visual relief. It showed the desire of people who wanted a better life and who tried to make the best of the worst of circumstances.

A faded blue train ran right through Kibera. It surprised me how close people stood to the tracks and how close they built their homes to them. Perhaps their everyday life was already so full of danger that a train outside their front door posed less risk compared with what they had to endure in the rest of the slum. More likely, there was just no other place to exist, and living right outside train tracks was the best they could do.

The brown water running through one of the creeks matched the colour of the roofs. Plastic bags littered the banks on either side. Piles of garbage had filled it up so much in Kibera that a person could walk almost all the way down the creek without getting their feet wet. Garbage lay everywhere on the street. Small children played on the trash-filled ground, unaware of the dangers of doing so.

The feeble houses looked as though one strong gust of wind could blow the whole slum down like a house of cards. People wore tattered clothes stained with dirt. Some of them looked so dirty, it was as if they just came out of a fire. In the distance, I saw bright children's clothes hanging on a clothesline. I loved seeing hope like this a slum. It indicated to me the desire of the parents in that family to give their children a future better than their own.

Antennas stretched up from many huts in an attempt to hear a word broadcast to them from the skies. People in search of hope, relief, and direction. I wanted to wrap my arms around Kibera in a comforting hug. People were hurting. They were suffering from poverty and a lack of opportunity. They were mentally, emotionally, physically, and spiritually sick. And they needed the gospel.

Just like anyone else.

People recognized our logo on the side of our bus—"Saving Children's Lives" printed at the bottom. I loved that saying so much that if I looked at it too long, I would begin to cry. As our bus came to a stop crowds of people began to gather. We smiled and greeted people as we stepped off the bus wearing our traditional bright orange T-shirts. Slums may look similar, but each slum is unique because the people are unique. And it was meeting each person that gave me so much joy.

We set up our tables to distribute food and clothing. The crowd sat down in the area in front of us. Mothers, fathers, children, singles. They came from different tribes and religions. But their faces, all crafted with individual beauty, shared the same look of desperation that comes to people who wonder from where their next meal is coming. Daddy once said there are rich people and there are poor people in the world. The rich are those who have enough food to last them until the next day. The poor are the millions and millions of others who go hungry, like those who had gathered before us.

Daddy addressed the people. He talked about trusting Jesus. About having faith in God. If God is able to create the entire world, He is able to take care of each one of us. He quoted from the Sermon on the Mount. *Look at the birds of the air, that they do not sow, nor reap nor gather into barns, and yet your heavenly Father feeds them. Are you not worth much more than they?*

We prayed for the food and handed out many meals to people. Daddy walked around asking people his favourite question: *Have you had enough to eat?* I handed out bread, smiling at people and giving them an encouraging word. "God loves you. Thank you for coming."

In the distance, I saw a girl, maybe she was 15, leaning against a post near one of the shacks. Her arms were crossed, her teeth clenched together, her eyes skeptical. She had a thin build, and her short hair was shaved nearly right to the skin. She wore a knee-length faded purple skirt that gave the impression it might have accompanied a happy girl when it was first bought new in some other country. Now it was owned by a girl whose dreams and hopes in life were anywhere but here. She wore a long-sleeved shirt that would have been white once but had since become a faded grey with all the twists and turns her life had taken.

As the lineup for food grew smaller, I saw her join the end. When her turn arrived, I offered her a piece of bread. She didn't meet my eyes. She stayed focused on the ground at her feet instead. I handed her slices of bread.

"May I join you?" I asked.

I sensed she wanted to leave. To just take her food and return to her life of worry. I could understand why. She was alone, even in a crowded slum. I imagined her going back to her hut and sitting there by herself.

I reached behind me for a bottle of water and handed it to her. She took it from me. She kept gazing down at the table. Then she raised her chin and looked at me. I recognized her eyes. They could have easily been mine from years ago.

She nodded. "All right," she said.

We sat down together on the ground.

"My name is Hannah."

She nodded again. Her eyes looked heavy, like she had not slept well, or at all. Her right arm had a bruise. She made no reply, and so I continued. "I am glad that you came here today."

Still nothing. But people often communicate most without saying anything. She had chosen to stay here, which told me everything I needed to know. At least for now.

"We are happy to have you here," I said. "And I want to tell you that—"

"Elizabeth," she said. "My name is Elizabeth."

"I am glad to meet you, Elizabeth."

She raised her eyebrows and focused her attention on the food in front of her.

"How has your day been today?" I asked.

She spoke nothing, which said volumes.

"Could I give you some food to give to your siblings? To your parents?"

She swished her bread around in her bowl, like she was trying to gather courage to speak. Instead of talking, I just waited. Silence can be a great healer.

She blinked a number of times. I knew that feeling all too well. She wanted to speak, needed to speak, but lived in that unsettling world of wanting to communicate but not having the faith to believe that the other person will care.

I did not interrupt her silence. She knew I was there. Knew I was listening. It was a test of sorts. Was I going to become disinterested in her by speaking about everyday things that did not matter? Or was I willing to honour her pain and wait among the commotion—to give her the assurance that there was nothing else in the world that mattered more to me now than my love for her?

She blinked again, rolling her eyes around to force out the grit and grime of the slum air that had mixed with the slightest onset of tears beginning to form.

Elizabeth stopped moving her bread. She breathed so lightly, I wondered if she was holding her breath. It was like she was gathering all the courage she could—like she was fighting a battle between running and staying.

She looked up at me. Her eyes bloodshot from the dust, the air, and her life. She watched me carefully. And I prayed that she would find in me the comfort she needed. Then, finally, "My parents are both dead," she said. She swallowed and then looked down, as if keeping her head up required too much energy.

The people talking and all the activity around suddenly seemed to quiet down, like someone had pushed a mute button to tune everything else out. Elizabeth and I remained in our little world.

"I understand," I said, almost whispering. It was all I could manage. I felt like I was staring at a younger version of myself.

Her expression changed. She looked up from her food. Her eyes told the story of a life filled with pain, confusion, and worry. She squinted ever so slightly.

"You?" Her voice was quiet, but strong. Her tone carried all the anger and hurt that had been built up inside her. "You understand me?"

I made no reply. I wanted her to know she could express herself to me.

I looked back at her with my heart. *Dear God, please help her see Your love for her in spite of her circumstances.*

"You think you understand me?" she said. "How could you possibly?"

She stood to her feet. I stood as well. I wanted to say something to help her. To keep her there, in our little world. But I wanted to give her room to reject me, too, if that's what she wanted.

Her eyes flared. "You have your nice family. Your good clothes. You have everything. How could you possibly understand me?"

She turned to leave. I knew in that instant I needed to respond. Needed to say something to continue construction on our bridge. She had asked a question. She deserved an answer.

She turned and took her first step away. This was it.

"Because my parents died too," I said.

She stopped. In that moment, I felt it all over again. It was like I was transported into my past. Reliving it all in slow motion. The passing of my birth mother, the passing of my birth father, the passing of my twin sister, Leah. It's impossible to hide that kind of hurt.

And I'm not sure I would have wanted to even if I could. Ironically, I hoped she could see it. All of it.

So there were stood. In a stalemate of sorts. She, looking into me. And I, into her.

I wondered how she would respond.

CHAPTER
twenty-nine

She studied my eyes, squinting again slightly, trying to figure out if I was telling the truth. I could not blame her. Her expression told me she had been lied to her whole life. She had reason for her mistrust.

"You are an orphan too?" she asked.

"I used to be."

"Used to?"

I nodded. "Would you like to sit down again? I would like to hear your story. I would like to listen to everything you would like to tell me."

She hesitated.

"It is all right," I continued.

Elizabeth stepped towards me. I sat down. She followed. Of the many battles to win, the first and perhaps most important is that she was willing to talk. That meant a lot to me. We sat down in the same spot and continued building our bridge. She from her side, and I from mine. Instead of looking at me, she looked over at Daddy Mulli. At how he interacted with people. How he cared for them. How he wore simple clothes.

"You first," she said.

That was fair.

And hard.

Don't tell your story. She won't believe you. And you have nothing to offer.

"All right," I said. It was far easier for me to be a listener than to be a talker. This was no exception. But she wanted to hear my story; and if telling her my life history would help, I was happy to do so.

"I grew up in Nyanza Province. Life was wonderful," I said with a smile. Too often I had thought about my tragic upbringing and not remembered enough the wonderful—truly wonderful—beginning that I had. It was a gift. It was excellent.

"It was the way life should be. But it did not last. My mother died when I was very young." I stopped speaking. I had to. That part never got easy. Not then. Not in all the years that followed. I bit my lower lip. She noticed. My eyes welled up with tears. I waited.

She did too.

Orphans understand.

I wiped my eyes.

"My father died shortly thereafter."

More tears. I did not bother wiping them this time. Perhaps she needed to see them. I, at the very least, still needed to feel them.

"My twin sister, Leah, after him."

If I was correct in reading her eyes, I saw the connection that came with speaking to someone who could affirm what she was feeling. What she was living.

The rest of the noise around us was drowned out completely. It was down to just her and me now in Kibera. Our hearts lay open to each other. And we shared in the relief that comes when you are sure the other person is not going to interrupt, lose interest, or try to solve your problem for you.

"And everything inside me shut down after that," I said. "I was not able or willing to speak with anyone. Everything hurt. And for years I felt like I was caught underwater in a current. I did not know up from down. Everyone and everything felt like they weren't really there. I was in unbearable pain, and I had no idea how to go about fixing it."

Her face softened. She didn't look afraid anymore.

"I felt I had no chance of anything improving in life. I was overcome with grief. And the scariest thing for me was that I had such a long way to go in life. I did not want to travel this journey in such sadness and fear."

She inched her head ever so closer to mine.

"And then I heard about Mully Children's Family. Daddy Mulli took me in. He gave me a bed in a safe place. I received food to eat. I got to go to school. I even got new parents. And about five hundred brothers and sisters."

She smiled. It was only brief, but it gave a glimpse into a truly humble, kind, yet downtrodden person. I thought about how to continue. But my thoughts became clouded with doubt.

Stop this. It's time to go. Look at all the work the others are doing. You should be helping them with the cleanup. It's not right for you to being doing this while the others work.

I steadied my mind. *Help me, Lord.*

"But everything changed when God revealed His love for me. All the fear I had left. I could suddenly open up to people. I received healing. Even though I did not understand everything, I was at peace."

Elizabeth tilted her head. She opened her mouth just slightly as if trying to inhale whatever had changed my life to make it part of her own.

"I pursued medicine. For years. And then it all came crashing down, and I felt like I was right back where I started. But that's when God changed the course of my life to do what I had always been designed to do. To listen to people and help them."

She took in a deep breath, then exhaled in an attempt to somehow rid her mind of all her pent-up worries and confusion. She thought a long while.

"This is true?" she asked.

"It is."

She glanced at Daddy Mulli. The sunlight reflected off her golden face. She looked down at the ground, and a tear rolled down her face and onto the dirt. And then, she stopped crying. I wasn't sure if it was her street-learned toughness that caused her to stop or if she had discovered the freedom that came with realizing she could allow herself to feel again.

"My parents died when I was young," she said. "I was lost. Totally. Completely. No one helped me. Any of us. I have been so confused. Just exhausted and worried ... until I met you now."

She swallowed. To me it seemed like it hurt her to do that, the way it hurts when you haven't eaten for a long time and you are getting used to food again.

"I used to have dreams, you know. I wanted to go to school. To study so that I could help people." She stopped. It was as if she had said too much already, and her mind was trying to comprehend what it was like to speak to someone else, instead of being forced to stay locked up inside her thoughts.

"But then everything changed," she said. "My dreams completely died." She did not need to say more. I understood. Perhaps too well. "There is something different about you. You have hope. Even though you had to pass through so much trouble."

I felt the last piece of the bridge going into place. We had each taken a chance. And now here we were. Together on the same bridge. Our bridge.

"Can I have the same hope as you?" she asked. "Is that possible?"

"It is."

"You are sure?"

"Yes."

"Can you tell me how I can have it too?"

"Sure," I said. "God loves you. He made you. Out of all the people in Kenya and in the whole world, He made you special. There is no one like you. But we have all sinned. The Bible says, for all have sinned and fall short of God's glory. That means that we have thought wrong thoughts and done wrong things. This separates us from God, who is perfect. We can never reach Him by trying to be good. There is nothing we can do to get back into relationship with God on our own."

"It is impossible?"

"Yes. For us to do it is impossible."

She tilted her head and squinted her eyes. I continued, "But with God, the impossible becomes possible. God sent His Son Jesus to the earth. He died on the cross in our place, then rose again from the dead. He took all our sins on Him. If we believe in Him, He will give us His eternal life. To live with Him in heaven forever."

"Me? I will live forever?"

"You can."

"How?

"Jesus said to repent and believe the Good News. Repent means to admit you are a sinner and that you cannot make your sins go away on your own. You want to turn away from your old life and turn to Jesus. Believing the Good News is believing that Jesus has paid for your sins and is offering you His eternal life. This is what has changed my life. This is what has given me hope and purpose in spite of everything I had to pass through."

"And this is possible for me?"

"It is," I said.

"How do you know this?"

"Because Jesus said that whoever believes in Him will not perish but have eternal life."

She looked out at the slum, deep in thought.

"You came here to Kibera?"

"Yes."

"Why?"

"For you."

"You are a good person. You are kind."

"Thank you. As are you." She raised her eyebrows. "This is my life story, and this is what I hope for you as well."

"Me?"

"Yes."

"And what do you hope for me?"

"That you would pray to ask God to make you His child."

She thought long and hard. I waited. I prayed.

"All right."

That was it. No big fanfare. Just two people in Kibera. One saved. One on their way.

"But I am not sure how to pray," she added.

"That is all right. I will pray, and if you agree you can repeat it."

Elizabeth nodded. She repeated after me.

"Dear God, thank You for creating me and for loving me. I admit I am a sinner. I turn away from my sin. I believe Jesus died in my place to pay for my sin and to give me eternal life. I put my faith in You only. No one and nothing else. I ask You to make me Your child. In Jesus' name, amen."

She and I opened our eyes. Hers looked clear and full of hope. She looked altogether different. I hugged her. I felt her hands grip my shoulders.

I felt like I was hugging Leah again.

The sunlight had begun to dim. In a few moments, it would be dark. We got to our feet. I hugged her again. I wished her a good night and told her I would see her again soon. The words Daddy Mulli had spoken to me earlier came back to me.

God will impact people through you.

Shortly after, Daddy rescued her and brought her to MCF Yatta.

I boarded the bus under the setting sun. I waved goodbye to Elizabeth. She smiled as she waved back. As we began our journey to MCF Ndalani, I started singing. The rest of the team joined me. The sound filled the bus. It felt so loud and full. Like a choir singing in a large church. It reminded me of the joy we had singing on the way to Tanzania.

The bus bumped over the potholes, shaking me back and forth. I glanced through the window at the passing blur of rusted houses. I thought about Elizabeth. About what it felt like to connect with her. I thought about the counselling program I had finished. And the medical degree I had not succeeded in pursuing. I thought about my incredible time at MCF so far. And I thought about my time before MCF. I felt something stirring inside of me. My mind was processing all I had experienced. It felt like the pieces of a giant puzzle coming together. At first I was unable to understand. Unable to connect what felt like disjointed pieces.

But then slowly the pieces did come together. It was like seeing the circle inside that square in math class all those years ago. The pieces of my life no longer seemed like random events. I began to see a pattern unfolding in my life. I gasped in awe.

And then, in that moment, everything became clear.

CHAPTER
thirty

The bus stopped outside the old devotional area at MCF Ndalani, in front of the house where Daddy and Mommy slept. It was a humble, quiet home. A lot smaller than the house they gave up in Eldoret all those years ago. Ironic that they moved from a bigger house to a smaller house, and yet their family grew many times larger.

I said good night to our teammates, to Daddy Mulli in particular. He smiled and wished me a good sleep. I have never quite been able to determine how he is able to provide so much hope with just the way he looks at me. And I think he sensed that. As I walked away, I turned back to see him. He gave a slight smile. He raised his hand. No words. They weren't necessary. I waved back at him. He walked in the direction of the school. A quiet man. A quiet spirit. Humbly going about, facing the impossible.

I looked back at the old devotional area. I remembered the way it used to look, with rickety wooden benches and a few working lights. I remembered where I sat that first night I arrived at MCF. I remembered what it was like to be with all my brothers and sisters for the first time. And what it felt like to see Daddy Mulli for the first time.

So much had happened since then.

And after all those years, for the first time I saw God's hand in everything. Like all the pieces of that puzzle were now put together, and I could step back and see it for what it was destined to be all along.

I often wondered and agonized over the first years of my life. My mother and father and my twin sister, Leah, had passed away. Hopelessness had gripped my soul. But then I came to MCF. I met Daddy and Mommy and discovered the joy and fun of being in such a big family. I learned about opening up to people and about being honest with my struggles and hurts. Then I repented and put my faith in Jesus. And His life changed me. He gave me real peace and purpose.

And I thought that purpose was for me to become a doctor.

But when that dream ended, I learned that I had a gift for listening to people. My heart loved to help people. I loved to give them my whole attention. I loved to be with them.

I loved to love people.

And it was my time in the Kibera slum with Elizabeth that finally taught me that everything in my life was completely by design. It was not random. It was not by accident. Even the hard things—especially the hard things—were used to reveal God.

How would I have been able to relate to Elizabeth if I had not been an orphan as well? She had been ready to walk away, and God used my story to encourage her. How would I have been able to listen to people's stories of pain if I had not been hurt as well? How would God have been able to give me His vision for my life if I hadn't known what it meant to come to the end of myself?

I was wrong about finding comfort in things being as they appear to be. The truth is that sometimes things are not what they appear to be. Being an orphan appeared hopeless, but God used my past to change someone else's future. Like a giraffe that can see higher and farther than all the other animals, I saw God use the deserts, mountains, and valleys of my life to bring about His purposes. Failing at medicine appeared to be the end. But, in fact, it was the beginning.

In His wisdom, God used MCF to rescue my sister Zemira and me. Like all my hundreds of brothers and sisters, she and I were given the opportunity—a second chance—to follow Christ while we were there.

I didn't want to spend my time doing anything else.

I looked up at the stars. They filled the darkness with so much brightness. They made it appear like it was not mostly evening with some light but rather that it was mostly light pushing away the small amount of darkness. They were scattered across the night sky in a dazzling display of beauty, swirls and spatters in a brilliant combination of formulas and artistry. I did not understand their pattern. I did not need to. I could still enjoy it. Admire it. Treasure it.

I knew there was a brilliant design behind them.

I hummed the song I had written. *I desire to walk with You. I desire to rejoice with You. I desire to live with You. Oh! Jehovah my Lord.* I remembered the sound of the choir when we sang in the classrooms late into the evenings. Evenings like this. Those times could have gone on forever. I suspected they would once I got to eternity.

I closed my eyes. Stretched out my arms. Took in a deep breath. I smelled the trees around me, each giving their unique scent. I wanted to give MCF a big hug. The people. The land. Daddy and Mommy. God, especially.

Every person has their reason why they love the place they call home. For me, the reason I loved MCF, the reason I held the people so dear, was because everything there felt like a taste of heaven.

No doubt there were many times when it did not seem that way. So many times I was tested. So many times I felt all was lost.

Faith is believing God is in control, even when everything seems out of control.

I entered my dorm and sat down on my bed. I held my blue-and-white Bible in my hands. In the quiet of the night, I thought about the day. About my time at MCF. About my life. God had pieced everything together. Put it all in its proper place. Organized everything in such a way that gave me peace. At times, it seemed like total chaos. Like everything had gone completely out of control. But looking back, it was genius design. This gave me hope moving forward. Hope for what challenges lay ahead. Hope for being able to help the people God would put in my path. I did not know what was coming. I did not know what new things were still to be learned. But I did know that when things do not seem to line up, God is still active. That He knows me. That He loves me.

And that God is working everything out to an excellent conclusion.

Even if at times we do not understand why things are happening.

AWARD WINNING TITLES BY
PAUL H. BOGE
AND
DR. CHARLES MUTUA MULLI

CASTLE QUAY BOOKS

The Man. The Miracles. The Mission.

FATHER TO THE FATHERLESS

The Charles Mulli Story

PAUL H. BOGE
Foreword by Bruce Wilkinson, *Dream for Africa*

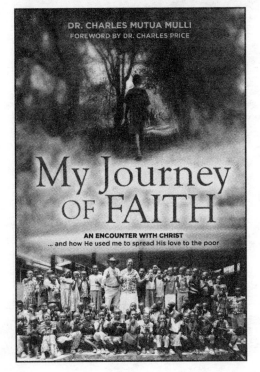

DR. CHARLES MUTUA MULLI
FOREWORD BY DR. CHARLES PRICE

My Journey OF FAITH

AN ENCOUNTER WITH CHRIST
... and how He used me to spread His love to the poor

THE BIGGEST FAMILY in the world

Written by Paul H. Boge   Illustrations by Faye Hall   Foreword by Grace Mutua

The Children. The Calling. The Compassion.

HOPE FOR THE HOPELESS

The Charles Mulli Mission

PAUL H. BOGE

Foreword by David Rowlands

Introduction by H.E. Hon. Daniel Arap Moi, Second President of the Republic of Kenya